DAILY RITUALS
for
HAPPINESS

How to be happy, every single day.

Lauren Ostrowski Fenton

Ostrowski House
The journey of life

Published by Ostrowski House Publications 2016

https://www.ostrowskihouse.com

Copyright 2016 © Lauren Ostrowski Fenton

The moral right of the author has been asserted. All rights reserved. No part of this book may be reproduced or transmitted by any person or entity, including internet search engines or retailers, in any form or by any means, electronic or mechanical, including photocopying (except under the statutory exceptions provisions of the Australian Copyright Act 1968), recording, scanning or by any information, storage, and retrieval system without the prior written permission of Ostrowski House Publications.

Editor Caitilin of Artful Words (www.artfulwords.com.au)

Cover Design by Damonza www.damonza.com

For Mum and Dad

This book is dedicated to my dear mum and dad. Dad, thank you for teaching me how to see happiness in ordinary day-to-day experiences and to recognise the importance of ritual. Mum, thank you for teaching me the resilience to get back up, time and time again.

About Daily Rituals for Happiness

Written by Lauren Ostrowski Fenton, Daily Rituals for Happiness is a user-friendly guidebook that teaches readers a step-by-step technique for experiencing happiness every single day. Focusing on ritual as the key to happiness, the book details the significance of these simple yet powerful practices and explores how they help instil a sense of self through reinforcing values, affirming connections to the community, and supporting wellbeing. Through insightful exercises in each chapter, readers are encouraged to develop self-awareness and create their own rituals, with an emphasis on feeling sensations of comfort, experiencing meaningful engagement, and embracing the rewards which come with planning and achieving realistic goals. The book provides support and encouragement for those who feel lost, lack motivation, and are searching for a straightforward and sustainable method to feel happy every day. Interwoven throughout is the beautiful story of the special relationship between Lauren and her father, Leonard Sergiusz Ostrowski, a Polish World War II survivor who emigrated to Australia, bringing with him his recipe for family, resilience, celebration and being happy.

Contents

About Daily Rituals for Happiness v

Introduction Discovering the keys to happiness xi

Chapter 1 Begin where you are 1

Chapter 2 Self-awareness is the key to happiness 37

Chapter 3 Create space for happiness 85

Chapter 4 Develop your rituals 133

Chapter 5 Practice daily 189

Chapter 6 Celebrate your progress 229

Conclusion The end of the story 261

Acknowledgments 277

About The Author 279

References, suggestions and more goodies for you 281

You, are so much bigger than what 'he said' or 'she said' but only if 'you say'. We each have infinite potential. Simply be yourself. Next time someone labels you as different, be proud. No one ever became a leader, created something new, thought of a new idea or stepped beyond their comfort zone by being the 'same'. Resist the sheep mentality and be different and CREATE, STRIVE, and ACHIEVE

Lauren Ostrowski Fenton

Introduction

Discovering the keys to happiness

I AM SITTING on the couch with my children all around me. They are dancing and singing and smiling. There are dress-ups, imaginary props and masks. Several interactions are happening simultaneously. My two boys are squashed together on a computer chair, singing off-key and a little too loudly. My younger daughter is holding one hand up, deftly videoing herself as she pretends to be a princess. My elder daughter is seated beside me, legs drawn up underneath her and a Mona Lisa smile on her face. She leans over, kisses my cheek and whispers, "We don't need anyone or anything. We are happy just as we are, Mum."

I feel tears in my eyes. The last several years have at times been really hard. My marriage has ended and I have lost my home, my business and my beautiful yoga studio. And with these losses went many of my traditions and familiar comforts. My core beliefs about who I was and how my world 'should be' have been shattered. I have felt lonely, empty and sometimes like a complete failure. Yet here I am, sitting on the couch surrounded by laughter and feeling happy.

Introduction

In times to come, I know I will not remember the bills that need to be paid, nor the occasions when I have depended upon donations of food. I will forget that I could not afford to buy my daughter a pair of school shoes and the days when our meals have been purchased with loose change. But I will always remember the glorious mayhem of our family happiness at this moment.

Yes, I am happy. And you can be too.

Are you feeling stressed, disillusioned or even a little lost? Are you sad or angry or discouraged? Maybe your life has not worked out like you planned or you have reached a crossroad and you don't know what to do next. You could be tired, confused or just plain overwhelmed, and it's possible that the thing you are thinking right now is "You don't know me. You don't know anything about me. How can you help me learn to feel happy?" Let me assure you, my friends, I do know how you feel. I have been there too. When my marriage ended, I couldn't imagine ever being really happy again, and to be honest, I resented being told by people to cheer up. I mean, what would they know?

If you are thinking the same thing about me now, then I want to tell you this. My path back to happiness was not an easy one, but rather a process which I learned over time. As much as I longed to discover some quick fix solution to find happiness and live without emotional pain, it just did not happen for me that way. I'm sorry to disappoint you, but that is not how it will work for you either and that is not what this book is about. Instead, I want to take you through a process that will help you focus on finding and feeling happiness in the moment. It will encourage you to notice the happiness that is already around you and within you, and it will support you in becoming more self-aware and self-accepting. Your experience will be different to mine, but I have seen how well this process works. Does it sound like something you would like to try? I hope so, because I really believe it can make a huge difference to you.

Where it all began

I'm Lauren, by the way, and I am really glad you are reading this book. It means that you are willing to make changes in your life to become a happier person, and that is a wonderful thing. It is not an easy journey that you are embarking upon, but I want to assure you that you are not alone. I will be with you, supporting you and cheering for you all the way. You already know that I am a single mum to four young children, including identical twin boys. I am also a counsellor, meditation teacher, and personal trainer. I have a popular YouTube channel called Lauren Ostrowski Fenton and a podcast called 'Being Well with Lauren'.

As you can probably already tell, I am passionate about wellbeing. I have written this book to share with you the story of how I found happiness through the practice of certain rituals. I call these rituals my daily happiness practice. This has been so life-changing for me that I really want to guide you through the process of developing your own daily rituals for happiness. I learned a lot about rituals through studying anthropology at university, but my fascination with them began long before that. It has a lot to do with the way I was brought up and with what I learned from my parents.

One of my stand-out childhood memories is of a family shopping trip to a local supermarket. As we wandered through the shop, loading groceries into our trolley, I recall my father cupping his hands to his mouth and calling out "I love you" at the top of his voice to my mother who was in the next aisle. Believe me when I tell you that this is *not* the way most

Introduction

Australians behave in public, let alone in supermarkets, yet I don't remember feeling embarrassed or self-conscious at the time. For me, such demonstrations of love from my father to my mother were simply part of ordinary life.

I grew up in outer Melbourne in Australia, the eldest of six children. My father was a self-made Polish immigrant and my mother was an educated, hard working Australian. Both were practicing Catholics and, as my father's behaviour in the supermarket shows, they were very much in love. Our family life was peppered with happy rituals, laughter and togetherness, from our traditional Polish Christmas to Dad reciting with me my maths times tables on the way to school each day. I remember with special fondness our family outings to the Polish bakery in Acland Street, St Kilda. Dad, who had never been one for moderation, would buy cardboard boxes bursting with cakes and donuts, and we would feast upon them, sitting around the table together. Years later, my sister nostalgically refers to these joyous feasts as the family 'pig outs'.

There was something about Mum's ritual chastising of my father's extravagance, shaking her head and whispering in Polish *"Nie tak duzo"* ("Not so much") which contributed to my sense of comfort and predictability. My mother learned to speak Polish fluently. She would cook traditional Polish meals and follow various Polish cultural rituals out of her love for my father. These rituals became the backbone of our happy family life. Somehow I felt that as long as we could continue to come together to celebrate, laugh, and converse through rituals, we would have the resilience to cope with life's hardships and enjoy life's celebrations.

In many ways, rituals like the ones I grew up with help make our lives flow more easily. They can support our wellbeing and our sense of self, and they can create a feeling of belonging to family or a community. The anthropologist Bronislaw

Malinowski (1922, 1926, 1944, 1976) suggested that people are more likely to turn to rituals when they face situations where the outcome is important or beyond their control. He theorised that when we are overwhelmed by hardship, rituals can help us create a positive state of mind. I have certainly found that to be true in my life, although I didn't realise it at first. In fact, my first experience of my happiness practice occurred almost by accident.

The keys to my happiness

After my marriage ended, I just felt so broken. Not only was the family unit shattered, but it felt as if I had failed at life. I was paralysed with fear, not knowing how to galvanise myself or which way to go. I had lost the sense of belonging that I had enjoyed in my childhood. I felt incredibly sad and was desperate for something that would offer me a little peace in my storm. I searched for signs of comfort, predictability and peace. I started to notice how much I looked forward to my morning cup of tea. The moment I woke up, I hopped out of bed, put my warm slippers on and trotted straight to the kettle to make my morning brew. That first sip of strong English breakfast tea in my favourite cup with the picture of kangaroo paw flowers on it was just wonderful. It was as if, for that moment, time stopped still for me and nothing else existed. And then I started to realise that nothing else did exist at that time, other than that moment of quiet in which I simply sipped my tea and enjoyed the feeling this experience brought me.

The immense comfort I received from this ritual activity got me thinking about the importance of noticing other little things. I realised that it was not just the act of drinking my morning tea that comforted me, but also the preparation of the tea, the anticipation of tasting it, the symbolism of using my favourite porcelain cup and the way that cup felt beneath my fingertips. There was a feeling of wellbeing that 'noticing' the experience gave me. I began to see that noticing was a skill in itself. With time, I found that I could train my mind to increase the cognitive pleasure and comfort I experienced from observing small things, much like when one learns to use a muscle efficiently. As a runner trains his or her body and increases cardiovascular fitness, so I found I could train my mind to increase my 'happiness' fitness. The more I flexed my happiness muscles, the stronger they became. And the more I anticipated and noticed my morning tea ritual, the more happiness the experience gave me.

Once I opened myself to noticing in this way, I began to explore the beliefs, values and behaviours around a range of other comforting habits and rituals. Gradually, I allowed myself to feel happiness through commonplace actions and patterns which I repeated each day. This experience of happiness was in the beginning so small that it was barely noticeable, but step by step and day by day, I started to notice more happy moments. In the beginning, I felt only mildly comforted. Then this mild sensation of contentment progressed to a general lifting of my mood until eventually it became a clear and sustained feeling of elation, which continues to grow even now.

I remember so clearly the moment when I realised that I alone held the keys to my own happiness. I was standing on a beach on the beautiful Mornington Peninsula in Australia, watching my twin boys play while I waited for my daughters to finish their Girl Guide meeting at the local hall. The beach was beautiful, covered with white sand and interesting shells. The boys ran along the sand from one shell to another, waving their arms, screaming with delight, gathering the shells and holding them up to the light. Suddenly they stopped and looked out towards the bay. Joining hands, they walked in unison into the water. With their backs towards me they stood knee-deep in the sea, silently looking towards the horizon. It was as if time simply stopped. I stood behind them, my pockets jammed full of sandy shells, listening to the lap of the waves and the sounds of the seagulls flying overhead. I could see my beautiful boys and feel the breeze across my face. My toes dug into the sand and I could smell the sting of salt air. It was wonderful.

In that moment, full of awareness and wonder, I realised *yes, this is it. This is happiness.* No book I read, no research I found, no philosopher's words and certainly no soulmate could give me this feeling, no matter how hard I searched. That is because it was here all along, within me. Happiness wasn't hiding from me. In fact, it was always with me and part of me. I just didn't know how to feel it. I didn't know how to really be happy. I often look back on that experience now, of seeing my boys holding hands on the beach. I have photos of that moment which I treasure and reflect upon. I replay in my mind the sounds of the ocean. I imagine again the aroma of the salty air as I feel the breeze brush my face. My previously untapped ability to notice – really notice – the gifts around me and to be fully present, fully aware, with genuine self-acceptance and a way of attuning my mind and my attention towards positive feelings is where I at last discovered my happiness. The next thing was to find a way that I could do this every day.

Why rituals matter

I have mentioned already how a lot of my journey of learning to be happy every day was built upon a foundation of rituals, and indeed much of our daily life is made up of rituals. These may be individual, family, religious, social or cultural rituals. Birthdays help us feel acknowledged and connected to our family and community. Weddings mark the commitment of two people, celebrating their love and devotion to each other. Blessings over food remind us to feel gratitude. Prayers or mantras affirm our good intentions, spiritual connection, and our need to feel compassion. In these ways, rituals celebrate both our sense of self and our sense of humanity.

What rituals hold in common is that they are about:
- acknowledging our sense of self
- reflecting our core values
- affirming our sense of worth
- instilling a sense of social belonging.

From the child who craves the familiarity of a soothing bedtime routine to an adult who enjoys going to the same café at the same time on the same day each week to sit in the same place and order the same thing, rituals provide us with the opportunity for both comfort and growth. They can help us practice gratitude and compassion, reinforce resilience, enrich the meaning and commitment within our relationships, encourage us to become more empathetic, and can enable us to develop cognitive behaviours that will enhance our self-esteem, social belonging and wellbeing.

I believe that many of us have been looking for happiness in the wrong places. Through practicing simple rituals and feeling the present moment, we can discover that the power to feel happy lies within us. Harvard researcher Matt Killingsworth (2012) says that being fully immersed in the present is more likely to bring happiness and "mind wandering" (away from the present moment) is "likely a cause and not a consequence of unhappiness". I find it fascinating that a distracted mind can cause unhappiness, especially when we can use rituals to stop our minds wandering and help us stay focused on the joy and comfort of the present moment.

A ritual for happiness can be understood simply as a set of predictable behaviours or series of actions which are undertaken with intention and provide feelings of comfort, engagement and reward. Essentially, these rituals help us feel good, but they can do much more than that. Through rituals, we have the power to unlock the truth of who we are and to learn to see the world in an entirely different light. They can help us develop awareness, compassion, gratitude and respect both for ourselves and for others. I have been doing my rituals for a long time, but as I further explored them during the writing of this book, I found that I became closer to God, saw the beauty in my parents, strengthened my relationship with those around me, and could even let go of resentment I had held on to since childhood. And there is a pleasant twist to this story, which I had not initially expected when I first started writing. It will unfold in the coming chapters. (Shh, no spoilers!)

Essential concepts

Before we get started, I want to introduce you to some essential concepts that I will be referring to throughout the book. I have already hinted towards some of them and they underpin the discussion and exercises that follow. These concepts are:

- the journey
- ways of seeing
- the art of noticing
- reflection
- practice.

The journey

In my thinking and my own self-exploration, I often use the term 'journey'. I have used this in my YouTube presentations and on my podcast, as well as when I am debriefing with the kids. This idea of the journey is really a key factor in our understanding of happiness because it places importance upon the process rather than the end result. The image of our journey also puts the responsibility back onto us. *We* decide to take each step and *we* navigate our own path. It really is, as the saying goes, all about the journey rather than the destination, but we are so conditioned to focus on the future, on goal setting, on saving for a rainy day, on having directions for how to get there that we forget the importance of what is happening to us and what we are doing right here and right now.

Let me give you an example. My children regularly attend an awesome, life-changing camp with fun activities that focus on bringing kids together to increase their self-esteem and resilience. My children often tell me that attending this camp is the highlight of their year, but despite the rewards it brings, I find all the packing and preparation for it can drive us all a little crazy. This year, as we packed and sorted and prepared, I stopped the kids to talk about what the camp was really about, why they enjoyed it and what it meant to them. I focused their attention upon the importance of the packing we were doing right then and how this was part of the overall adventure. I reminded them that the packing is, in fact, part of the journey.

So it is with life. Happiness is not about arriving at some imaginary 'happiness camp'. Rather, it is about enjoying the process of packing for and travelling towards happiness (and maybe even getting lost once or twice along the way.) That's why I talk about happiness as a journey, complete with ups and downs, the good times and the bad. It is all part of happiness.

Reading this book and choosing to take responsibility for your own happiness is part of your journey. Often, the learning that comes with making such changes in your life can be confronting. That's why it is really important to be kind to yourself along the way, to embrace your progress and enjoy the journey itself.

Ways of seeing

If you have been reading closely, you might have noticed that I have already used the phrase 'ways of seeing' in reference to our perspective or view of the world. This concept of a way of seeing is integral to our ability to feel happy and it also applies to the way in which we may practice certain rituals to help us feel happier. We each have a set of custom-made glasses through which we see our world. Our way of seeing involves:

- the values and beliefs we hold
- our sense of self-awareness and self-acceptance
- the way we choose to perceive the experiences in our lives (and we do have a choice about this)
- how we allow these experiences to shape us.

From the moment we are born, we are exposed to experiences and these include relationships and events. These relationships and events mould our lives and affect the window through which we see our world. Although our experiences may essentially seem to be happy or not so happy, we choose whether to take these on as part of who we are and internalise them, and we can also choose whether or not to let them go. From childhood through to adulthood, we are like backpackers, shouldering the luggage of our lives, choosing what to carry with us and what to leave behind. We see our world and walk the journey of our lives affected by the emotional baggage we carry. Once you become aware of your way of seeing, you are better equipped to understand and reinvent yourself by changing your patterns of perception and occasionally emptying your emotional backpack. Now, a word of warning here. It took me close to five years to see that my backpack was unnecessarily full. Go easy on yourself. It may take you a little while to empty your own backpack Perhaps you may need to carry it with you for a little longer, and that is ok. Perhaps you may be able to lighten it gradually over time. This is your journey, so walk it at your own pace.

The art of noticing

Another important concept, which follows on from ways of seeing, is 'the art of noticing'. This is about paying attention, observing and witnessing every detail of your life in order that is more fully experienced. I have personally found that the more I practice the art of noticing, the more positive and optimistic my way of seeing has become. Why don't you take a moment right now to notice what is going on around you? What sights, sounds and aromas can you detect? How does it feel to breathe the air? Pay attention to your breath and notice the exhilarating gift of inhaling and exhaling.

Walk around the area you are in, whether it is your bedroom, the kitchen, your office or the garden. Touch things, feel their texture, and listen to what you can hear. Notice one sense at a time for several moments and then go on to another sense and notice this for several moments too. Listen to sounds, one at a time. Separate out the various aromas and observe them one by one, naming each of them in your mind. Notice how you feel about each sense and try not to let your mind wander or jump forward into the future. As soon as you let your mind leap into the future, you lose this precious moment. You are in charge here. You get to choose where you allow your mind to go. You have the power to keep your mind in the present, in the here and now.

The ability to quieten your thoughts and to practice the art of noticing what is going on around you lies within your mind, and the ability to change and modify your behaviour goes hand in hand with it. Throughout this book, we will complete a number of exercises to help you practice the art of noticing. For now, I just want you to register that 'noticing' is a skill. It is one we can consciously develop and it can help us feel happier.

Reflection

Learning to reflect on ourselves, our experiences, our behaviours and our choices is so important when it comes to being happy. For example, reflecting upon happy memories can help bring peace to the present. There are many ways we can develop our ability to reflect. Two of my favourites are meditation and journaling. We will be learning more about both of these in the coming pages. The important thing about reflection is that it opens our minds to the precious gift of perspective. When we look back on our lives and experiences from a place of calm consideration, we can begin to see events in a new light. We are better able to cultivate an attitude of forgiveness and compassion, both towards ourselves and towards others. Of course, reflection can sometimes lead to unhealthy rumination and recrimination. That is where meditation can be so helpful. It may take some practice, but in time you will develop the skills to reflect with detachment.

Practice

Did I say 'practice'? When I was young I practiced the piano every morning at 6 a.m. I would wake my poor parents with my disjointed sounding piano scales as I warmed up my fingers for Chopin and other favourite composers. I especially loved 'Für Elise' by Beethoven. I found that unless I preceded my playing with daily piano scales, my fingers became stiff and I could not play with the same familiarity and harmony. The daily practicing of piano scales reminded my fingers how to feel and understand music. In some ways, this concept is what this whole book is about. You can only understand your way of seeing if you practice understanding it. And you are more likely to 'feel' happiness if you practice doing so. The way to develop the art of noticing is also by practice. And, as I noted above, learning to reflect with kindness and insight takes practice. This idea of practice also links back to the idea of the journey, because this is not about achieving perfection. It is about doing it anyway, every day, because the benefit is in the doing and in the meaning behind the practice. A ritual is only a ritual if it is practiced. In some ways, you could say that happiness itself is a practice. But practice takes dedication. That is why the exercises in this book are designed to help you build that dedication to your practice.

Here is what I believe

Now that you know the core concepts we will explore in this book, I want to introduce some of my ideas about happiness. I have touched on a few of these already and we will delve into this topic in more depth in the next chapter. What is important for you to know is that every change and decision we make is preceded by a belief. That's why I want to share with you my beliefs about happiness in general and about your happiness specifically. These beliefs have been instilled in my mind over time. They are the result of hard thinking and hard learning, and they inform my approach to happiness in this book. What I believe is this:

1. *Happiness is a state of mind* that you can only feel today, not yesterday nor tomorrow. If you look for happiness in the future, you risk being perpetually unsatisfied, like a donkey forever following an elusive carrot that is suspended on a rod from his forehead.

2. *Happiness is an individual, subjective experience*, which means that only you will know what happiness is for you at your age and stage of life. No one can tell you where to find or how to feel your happiness, because it is yours and yours alone.

3. *Happiness requires self-awareness*, and with awareness comes understanding, acceptance and development, because it is simply not possible to be happy if you are not happy with who you are.

4. *Happiness may be experienced in three ways* and these are through feeling comfort, having engaging empathetic relationships, and having rewarding goals. These will all be explored in more detail in the chapters that follow.

5. *Happiness requires a conscious decision and intentional action*, so you need to make the decision to feel happy in spite of, or perhaps inspired by, the events in your life. You also need to commit to acting in certain ways to bring happiness into your life, no matter what gets thrown at you.

6. *Happiness takes skill and practice*, just like my piano playing. If you want to enjoy the music of life, you need

to practice and develop your skills in doing this. That is where your rituals come in.

The journey ahead

How are you feeling, my friends? We have already begun to look at a lot of important ideas and we are still only in the Introduction. I hope you are excited about your journey ahead. Let me give you an idea of what you can expect. This book is divided into six chapters, through which we will explore issues relating to both happiness and rituals. In each of the chapters, you will find exercises that are designed to help you learn more about yourself and to enable you to develop your own happiness practice. You will also find parts of my own story, including more about my realisation of happiness through ritual.

Chapter 1 begins by inviting you to reflect on where you are right now. It asks you to consider whether you are ready to commit to making a positive change in your life. In **Chapter 2**, we look at the importance of self-awareness, self-understanding and self-acceptance to your happiness, while **Chapter 3** focuses on creating the physical, mindful and social space for happiness and your ritual practice. At the heart of the book is **Chapter 4**. Here, you will be introduced to a range of rituals for daily happiness and be invited to develop your own ritual practice. **Chapter 5** is full of information to help you consolidate and maintain your happiness rituals so you can enjoy practicing them, even when life gets challenging. Finally, **Chapter 6** is all about celebrating your progress. You'll be invited to reflect on your journey, rejoice in the present moment and look forward to your happier, healthier future. I can't wait to get started, but there is one more thing I want to share with you before we get going.

Create your own happiness

I believe that through reading this book, completing the exercises and developing your own daily rituals for happiness, you will learn more about yourself and how you can become happier. Make no mistake, however. As I have pointed out above, being happy takes effort and dedication. It is up to you to decide if you are willing to do the work. I may hand you the canvas, but ultimately you are the artist and you are the only one who can paint your own masterpiece. So, are you ready to learn how to be happier? The best place to begin your journey is where you are right now.

An important note

I have written this book as a guide for all of us, even me. The language I have used is suitable for teenagers as well as adults. In fact, a lot of the exercises in the book have been developed and practiced by my own family. But please note that this book is not aimed at those who are experiencing clinical depression, anxiety, trauma or loss. Life is so precious, my friends. If you feel severely unhappy or anxious, please always seek professional support.

Chapter 1
Begin where you are

It is not the journey TOWARDS a happy self.
The journey is BEING a happy self.

AS A CHILD, I was lovingly nicknamed the What If Girl by my parents because I was always wondering about what may or may not happen and what I would do about it if it did. I ruminated endlessly over all the possible eventualities that could occur. In my head, I was perpetually living in the future and somehow life appeared to be a whole lot better there than it was in my present. I believed that *when* I fell in love I would be happy. I believed that *when* I bought a house, *when* I found my dream job, and *when* I had just enough money, my life would be complete. Finally I could tick the happiness box. Case closed. The story would end and I would live happily ever after. I know differently now.

After my marriage ended, one of the first important lessons I learned about happiness was not to wait to be rescued. In order to feel happy again, I knew I could not just sit around hoping for some quick fix or gimmick to solve all my problems.

Chapter 1

I also realised that I had to stop being the What If Girl who lived in future possibility. Instead, I had to live my real experience and learn to become the Begin Where You Are Now Person. I needed to stop expecting anything or anyone to hand me my happiness. In that watershed moment of realisation, when I watched my beautiful boys holding hands and standing knee-deep in the ocean, it became so clear to me that happiness is a 'feel it now' state and it's one I could choose. Beginning where you are and understanding that happiness is a state you can decide to be in is what this chapter is all about.

We're going to dive straight into the question of what happiness really is and consider what it means to us as individuals. We will learn about what determines our happiness and how we can start to notice it more in our lives. I'm going to explain more about the three ways in which I believe we can experience happiness, and you will be invited to relate these ways to the things you already do. We will begin to think about rituals too, and how our activities can become part of our daily happiness practice. I will tell you how this works by explaining one of my favourite and most fundamental rituals that you can use as well. Finally, you will get started with your first, simple ritual for happiness.

We are right at the beginning of our happiness journey and I want you to know that I will be with you every step of the way. It may be that your life feels unfair to you right now. Perhaps you have experienced misfortune or unreasonable judgment or have been marginalised in some way. This could make even the idea of feeling happy seem pretty challenging to you. You may have been the victim of bullying or abuse or injustice, and that's why you don't feel ready or able to take responsibility for your own happiness. Perhaps you feel it's too hard right now. Perhaps you feel you just can't do it. Maybe later. Maybe when… Ok, now take a moment and just breathe. I get it.

I understand your hesitation and your fears, my friends. I have felt it too. But let me tell you this: there is no perfect time to start your happiness journey. There is only now.

Happiness begins where you are, so let's get started.

What is happiness?

The French Buddhist monk Matthieu Ricard (2004), named as the happiest man in the world, said that if something is going to determine the quality of our lives, then we had better know what it is. It sounds like such a simple question, doesn't it, to ask: What is happiness? Surely we could just look up the word 'happiness' in a dictionary and find a reasonable answer? No, not so. Indeed, psychologist Daniel Kahneman (2010) suggests that the word happiness is too simple to describe the true complexity of this state of mind. I think it is only in recent years that we are beginning to scratch the surface of happiness, and we are also slowly starting to understand that many of us may have been looking for it in all the wrong places (Gilbert, 2005; Roberts, Tsang & Manolis, 2015). I used to believe that happiness came from external relationships, events and objects, so that is where I looked for it. I looked beyond and outside myself for the perfect relationship, the ultimate occasion, or the best possession I could buy. Would you be surprised to learn that I did not find happiness there? It seemed I had to search elsewhere instead.

When I commenced my happiness journey, I wanted to know everything about the topic. I wanted to understand all the research, read all the books, know all the behaviours of happy people, consider all the strategies that help people to be happy, and delve into all the philosophies and theories behind happiness. I wanted to understand what happiness looked like, how it behaved, and indeed what it had for breakfast. I was like a 'happiness groupie'. I began by combing the internet, looking for everything I could find on happiness. This led me to explore the works of such wonderful people as Aristotle, the Dalai Lama, Martin Seligman, Albert Ellis, Eckhart Tolle, William Glasser, Matthieu Ricard, Matt Killingsworth, Sonja Lyubomirsky, Deepak Chopra, Wayne Dyer, Fritz Perls, Daniel Gilbert, Gretchen Rubin, Brené Brown, Shawn Achor, Daniel Kahneman, Malcolm Gladwell, Ron Gutman, Graham Hill and many more. (I have placed a list of my favourite resources on happiness at the back of this book. Enjoy!)

As some people may watch with fascination and delight the popular sitcom series *Friends*, so I watched transfixed as these speakers shared their experiences and research on happiness in TED Talks. Late at night, after the kids fell asleep, I tucked myself up in bed under a warm doona with my lavender oils burning. I would flip open my Mac laptop, take a sip from a nice cup of tea and watch my version of *Friends*. Watching TED Talks, I spent time with the humorous yet insightful Dan Gilbert (2004), who speaks to the viewer as if he is lounging around with good friends at a Sunday barbecue and inspires us to recognise that our beliefs about happiness are often wrong. I listened, transfixed, to the brilliant Daniel Kahneman (2010), who examines the riddle of our moment by moment experience of happiness compared with our memory of happiness, and demonstrates that our experiencing self is often different to our remembering self. I enjoyed the fascinating, dry wit of Malcolm Gladwell (2004), who explores the nature of choice and happiness using the narrative of chunky pasta sauce sales. And I learned much from Matt Killingsworth (2011), who built an amazing app called Track Your Happiness and monitored in real time the happiness of 15,000 people from all over the world, only to discover that we are often happiest when we are in the moment, and that the more our mind wanders, the less happy we may be. As I heard these amazing speakers share their groundbreaking research, I began to develop my understanding of happiness and rituals.

Inspired by my discoveries, I also attended self-inquiry workshops, prayed, practiced yoga, meditated, went back to university to complete my Masters degree in counselling, and did a lot of soul searching. Initially I believed that if I researched hard enough, kept reading books and academic papers, and watched more and more TED Talks, the definition of happiness would become clear to me. In reality, I found that defining happiness is really quite challenging. Some of the popular information found on the internet and in the media used pictures of ageless beauty, beautiful houses and shiny cars, suggesting that happiness is to be found in accumulating wealth, finding a soulmate or gaining social recognition. Well, that all sounded reasonable to me. Other resources such as Eckhart Tolle advised that happiness is experienced more through self-discovery and letting go of attachment (Tolle, 2004; Ricard, 2003). Yes, I liked that approach too. Still more resources insisted that happiness comes to us via social connection, compassion and living a full and meaningful life (Dalai Lama, 2009). I certainly agreed with the notion of happiness being linked to a life with meaning.

There are, of course, some similarities and overlaps between these different philosophies. But the more I looked, the more I learned that there is an incredible diversity in opinions about what happiness actually is (Ricard, 2003). So which definition is right? With such variety, and sometimes such opposing views, how can any of us really know what happiness is? All I wanted was one simple answer and then I could simply follow the instructions and be happy. But, as I will share with you through the pages of this book, I began to understand that an easy approach to happiness is not always the most sustainable one. I realised that the life I thought I had came from my way of seeing it, rather than being based on an objective, hard-faced reality. Upon making that realisation, I recognised too that my way of seeing could be changed. That is when I started to see that happiness is like a diamond which is held up to the light. The spectrum of colours that lives within and sparkles from it changes depending on the way the light touches it. Ultimately, I am in charge and I choose how to hold the diamond of my life up to the light.

With time, I realised that no one has the power to hand me the ultimate answer to happiness because, like the colours in my diamond, my happiness lies within me and can only radiate from my own moment by moment experience. Happiness for me is all about 'being' – being present, being comfortable, being well, and being engaged with meaning. It is a deep sense of serenity and fulfilment that comes from self-acceptance, mental and spiritual health, and tranquillity. I define happiness as the ability to feel and truly notice comforting experiences, to maintain a sense of wellbeing, and to build meaning through relating to others and the world around me. And despite the challenges in my life, I can honestly say that I now experience this happiness every single day. Please believe me when I tell you that you can do so too.

What is happiness for you?

I have shared here how I feel about happiness, my friends, but my story is not your story and my experiences are not your experiences. As I said in the Introduction, happiness is an individual experience. I am happy and now I want to share my understanding with you, but it is up to each of us to find our own understandings and to know not only ourselves, but also our purpose, our direction and the ways we may feel happiness during different ages and stages of our lives. After writing several drafts of this book and going back repeatedly to my sources, I realised that it won't work for me to simply write about a one size fits all version of happiness, because happiness is about you, the individual.

Throughout the coming chapters, I will be asking you to stop, think, and even meditate on how you feel about yourself and the experiences in your life. Let's start with you taking a moment now to consider what happiness is for you. Consider the ways in which you feel happy. How are they working for you? Do they bring lasting effects? Are they sustainable? Where do you look when you are searching for happiness? Is it within or do you search somewhere outside yourself? Do you notice your experiences moment by moment? Do your ways of feeling happy bring you health, contentment and cause for celebration? Or do your current methods for feeling happy sometimes lead you into stress, distraction and fears about an uncertain future? Who are you when you are happy? What beliefs, values and behaviours do you follow at these times? What do you believe about happiness? Where have these beliefs come from? Are they your own or are they simply those that you have been told? Do they feel true to you? Do they support you?

Finding answers to these questions is an important part of your journey because, ultimately, your happiness is what you say it is rather than what someone else tells you. You call the shots here. We can throw around definitions and theories and philosophies of happiness until the cows come home, but in the end, you need to decide what happiness means and how it feels to you. My friends, the simple fact is this: nothing and no one can make us happy aside from ourselves. That means not only that we can decide what happiness means to us, but also that we can *choose* to be happy. Like I said in the Introduction, happiness is like a canvas that is ours to paint. We get to pick our own colours, paints, brushes and the method we'll use to create our masterpiece. Even more than this, we can also decide how we will view this canvas...knowing that our vision of it may shift over time.

Exercise 1: How happy am I each day? Happiness self-assessment questionnaire

So, what does your canvas look like right now? In keeping with our focus on beginning where you are, we are going to dive in to your first exercise. Each of the exercises in this book is based on the essential concepts outlined in the introduction. The exercises have been designed to guide you on your journey and to help you think about your ways of seeing. Some will also invite you to practice the art of noticing and encourage you to reflect. After each exercise, I will ask you to consider what you found valuable in it and also what you have learned about yourself. It is only when we know who we are that we can understand what makes us happy. Our self-awareness and self-understanding work hand in hand.

The purpose of this exercise is to help you get to know yourself so you can work out the areas in which to focus your happiness practice. There are, of course, many great happiness questionnaires out there, but this one is designed to get you thinking about your experience of happiness and reflect on your current beliefs about it. To help sort through some different ways of feeling happiness, I have placed a number of statements into four categories. Now this does not mean that these are the only categories these statements could be placed under, but it does give us a place to start. Please read through the statements below and indicate how much you agree or disagree with them by giving each one a number according to the following scale:

1. = strongly disagree
2. = moderately disagree
3. = slightly disagree
4. = slightly agree
5. = moderately agree
6. = strongly agree.

We are doing this exercise to explore how you feel about your life and how happy you are today, so I suggest you curl up in your favourite chair with a hot cuppa and complete the assessment. At the end of the book, I am going to invite you to revisit this questionnaire so you can compare how you feel and how you rate yourself after completing and practicing the happiness exercises and rituals you will learn on your journey.

Here we go!

Feeling comfort

1. *I feel happy most days.*
2. *I smile every day.*
3. *I engage in hobbies or interests which I enjoy.*
4. *I have daily rituals which I enjoy.*
5. *I have a sleep routine and I sleep well.*
6. *I eat a balanced, nutritional diet.*
7. *At the end of the day, I feel peaceful.*
8. *I am aware of experiencing comforting moments throughout the day.*
9. *I enjoy my daily walk or exercise.*

Chapter 1

Empathetic and engaging relationships

1. *I have several friends who I am close to.*
2. *I participate in my community.*
3. *I feel fortunate to have the relationships that are currently in my life.*
4. *I have boundaries and can say no if necessary.*
5. *I attend family celebrations and enjoy these occasions.*
6. *I enjoy meals at the table with friends or family each day.*
7. *I give to others.*
8. *I don't hold grudges.*
9. *I feel compassion for the people in my life.*
10. *I have several habits I repeat which give me a sense of connection with others.*

Experiencing rewarding goals

1. *I set rewarding and achievable goals.*
2. *I make time for meaningful things in my life.*
3. *I enjoy the present moment and don't get distracted.*
4. *I embrace change.*
5. *I acknowledge my achievements and make sure I celebrate them.*
6. *I have habits I repeat each day which I find rewarding.*
7. *I manage and structure my time.*
8. *I enjoy planning, anticipating and working towards my goals.*
9. *I enjoy consciously reflecting on happy times.*
10. *In most ways, my life is just the way I want it to be.*

Self-awareness

1. *I know my strengths.*
2. *I accept my weaknesses but continue to work on them.*
3. *When I make mistakes, I review them realistically, adjust my behaviour and move on.*
4. *I am happy with what I have now.*
5. *I make time each day to practice mindfulness, through prayer, meditation or simply being in the moment.*
6. *I rarely find my mind wandering.*
7. *I let go of negative experiences fairly quickly.*
8. *I don't ask for reassurance or worry about what others think of me.*
9. *I have rituals which give my life meaning.*
10. *I feel grateful for my life every day.*

How was that for you? Did any of your answers surprise you? Did you learn anything new about yourself? The interesting part of this questionnaire is that through rating the statements not only do you learn about your own happiness, but you also learn about your ability to notice and practice skills in happiness. Considering these statements also prompt you to think about your beliefs about happiness. You will remember that I mentioned my beliefs in the introduction. To recap, I believe happiness is a state of mind, happiness is felt individually and requires self-awareness, happiness may be experienced in three ways, happiness requires a decision and responding action, and it is founded upon a daily practice. Did this questionnaire help you uncover any of your beliefs about happiness?

Obviously the higher your score, the happier you may be,

Chapter 1

but let's put our scores aside for now and instead explore your findings as an opportunity for self-awareness, rather than seeing them as a pass or fail rating. When I first wrote this questionnaire, I thought a lot about different ways we could use the answers. I found there was so much juicy information here giving me an insight into who I am and what I could do differently. But right now, I want to keep it simple. While we could spend literally chapters analysing your answers, we are not going to do that. I want this book to be about moving forward in small steps and patting ourselves on the back along the way.

Completing this questionnaire may help you chart where you are now, understand your own sense of happiness, and establish where you need to focus more attention. It's kind of like doing a maths test and realising you need to focus more on fractions. When you pay attention to something, and give it a rating, you might find ways to improve it, shift your focus, or realise your strengths and limitations. After completing this questionnaire, I thought to myself, "I have a lot to be grateful for. I have awesome friends and family, but I probably need to focus more on exercises to reduce anxiety, learn to let go, and improve my sleep." This questionnaire helped me pinpoint the areas which may have been reducing my ability to feel happy every day. But remember this is a learning process, so go easy on yourself.

You will have noticed that I included a few references to fitness and wellbeing among the statements. If you follow my YouTube videos and my podcast, you probably know that this is a favourite topic of mine because I am a personal trainer and meditation instructor. Although I think that sleep and fitness are vital parts of happiness, we do not discuss these in detail in this book. We just want to focus on the importance of practice as a formula for happiness which may also be applied to other areas of your life. Teaching you to build a practice is kind of like giving you the seeds and the 'how to' manual for growing your own apple trees, rather than simply handing you a shiny apple.

Principles of learning

Speaking of teaching, don't you think that one of the most exciting things about our lives is that we are forever learning and evolving? It is all about developing a sense of self-discovery. To become aware of who you intrinsically are and to embrace your true self is a journey. Learning about happiness, and indeed just being happy, is an important part of this. It involves waking up to life, adapting our feelings and building our skills through practice and reflection. Learning is an organic process and each person learns at their own rate, so as you make your way through the lessons in this book, you may wish to take regular breaks, perhaps go for a brisk walk and breath in the air or do some gardening. After all, you can only remember so much at one time, so don't forget to pat yourself on the back and congratulate yourself along the way. Likewise, you may wish to re-read sections or take notes to help yourself remember. Remember, and this point is really important, you are more likely to learn about how to be happy through demonstration and developing a practice than through simply reading.

Let's take a moment now to reflect on what you have gained through doing this first exercise. I am going to ask you two questions and I have included an example response as a guide for you. I encourage you to fill in your own answers and use them for self-reflection and self-encouragement. All of these exercises and rituals, along with your reflections, can help you increase your self-awareness and ability to be in the now. They will enable you to step forward and develop your practice.

CHAPTER 1

What value did you find in this exercise?

My response: What I found most valuable about this exercise was that it helped me reflect upon the true meaning of happiness and how I can bring that meaning back to the present. It was interesting to note how there are so many areas of my life which are affected by happiness. I also learned that happiness is not about a rating but is about getting to know myself in the here and now.

Your response:

_____
_____
_____
_____

What did you learn from this exercise?

My response: When I initially did this exercise, I began to consider the core values of my happiness and how I may reinforce them. I also noticed that when I lacked self-respect, lacked social engagement, or may be down on myself; this affected my ability to be happy.

Your response:

_____
_____
_____
_____

What determines our happiness?

Equipped with this snapshot of our current level of happiness, we can begin to consider ways to enhance our experience of it. In my research for this book, I came across some interesting studies about our capacity to influence our own level of happiness. In one of these, Lykken and Tellegen (1996) used fascinating research into the nature of twins to show that the happiness of identical twins is more closely aligned than that of fraternal twins, which they argue means that happiness is genetic. Another interesting concept is the set point theory of happiness (Lucas, 2008). This is one of the founding theories of happiness and proposes that we each have a genetic 'set point' for happiness which is determined by our genetics and by our early childhood development. Set point theory suggests that about 50% of our happiness is determined by our genes and cannot be changed.

When I first read this, I was quite frankly appalled. Goodness me, I thought, do we really have so little control over our own happiness? Can our level of wellbeing truly be so preset and therefore beyond our control? On reflection, however, I realised that it is not as bad as it sounds. All is certainly not lost. These findings mean that there is still a lot of our happiness which is left up to us to control through our values, thoughts and behaviours. The wonderful thing about set point theory is that it gives an interesting spin to the idea of seeing the glass as half-full or half-empty. Are you discouraged to learn that about 50% of your happiness is genetically pre-determined and cannot be changed no matter what you do? Or are you happy to focus on the 50% control you have over your happiness and see it as being full of opportunity? After my initial shock, I decided to see the glass as half-full and embrace the 50% I have to play with. This whole book is about

Chapter 1

recognising that opportunity, working on that potential, and enhancing it with mind training and dedicated practice.

As a society we have been told through the media that happiness is about acquiring money, success, soulmates and heaps of shiny possessions. The media socialises us to desire the pretty things in life, rather than looking for sustainable solutions. Thanks to all this clever marketing, our happiness radar can be a little off, meaning that we may not recognise the potential we have to influence the 50% of happiness that is ours to play with. So what can we do to readjust this faulty radar? We can begin to pay attention to the things that genuinely make us feel happy and then do these with greater application, ceremony and ritual. We can learn to really feel and notice happiness.

Mihaly Csikszentmihalyi, a Hungarian professor of Psychology from Claremont Graduate University talks about realising happiness through developing what he calls 'flow' in regular, day to day activities. It is relevant to give you a little bit of insight here into Mihaly Csikszentmihalyi's (2004) background, as he had experiences in World War Two that are not unlike those of my father. Mihaly says: "I grew up in Europe, and World War II caught me when I was between seven and 10 years old. And I realized how few of the grown-ups that I knew were able to withstand the tragedies that the war visited on them – how few of them could even resemble a normal, contented, satisfied, happy life once their job, their home, their security was destroyed by the war. So I became interested in understanding what contributed to a life that was worth living."

Listening to this, I wondered if it is when we lose almost everything that has meaning to us that we realise it is the ordinary, day to day things which give us happiness. Mihaly decided to try to find where in people's 'normal experiences' could they be happy. He discovered that people are happiest when they are in a state of flow which is achieved when they focus with deliberation upon normal daily activities. It's all about noticing what is happening to us and applying ourselves and our attention to what we do.

Exercise 2: Noticing happiness

As we've discovered, it is often easier for us to believe that happiness is what others tell us it is, rather than reaching deep within ourselves and discovering what we really feel. In the beginning of my journey, I spent a lot of time in silence, just allowing myself some emotional space. I knew that I needed to reconnect with the core of who I am. I spent time writing, meditating, walking and watching nature. Slowly, slowly, I began to realise more deeply who I am and what makes me happy, but it took a lot of observation and self-reflection. For this second exercise, we are going to learn two techniques to help us develop the art of noticing our own happiness and help us to be in the present experience of life. Just as before, this exercise centres on the key concepts and my six beliefs as outlined in the introduction.

1. **Meditation**

I am going to start with one of my favourite practices: meditation. Now let me reassure you. Some of you may feel that meditation is a practice which involves spiritual or religious beliefs. If that is what it is for you, then great, but meditation does not have to be defined like that. To meditate means to engage in contemplation or reflection. It is simply the act of consciously observing your thoughts. It may also mean that you apply yourself to a mental task, such as focusing on your breathing or repeating a mantra such as "I can do it" in order to encourage positive cognitive change and greater awareness. Not only has meditation been intrinsic to my healing, but it

CHAPTER 1

has also allowed me to understand myself better, let go of the small stuff and clear my mind. Let's give it a go now.

For this self-awareness meditation exercise, I invite you to sit quietly on a chair with your feet on the floor, or to sit on the floor with your legs crossed. Make sure your back is straight, your shoulders are down, your neck is long, your rib cage is wide, and you can breathe comfortably. Now, as you settle into your body, begin to focus on your breath as you inhale and exhale. Visualise your breath entering and exiting your lungs through your nose. Imagine the journey of your breath and the repetition of this journey. I want you to particularly notice the repetitions of inhalations and exhalations. Find comfort in the predictability of the act of breathing, but don't place any expectation upon yourself. At times you may find your mind wandering away. Don't worry about this. Just gently bring your mind back to the repetition of your breath.

As you settle into this visualisation of the pathway of your breath, begin to gently lengthen your breathing. Breathe in slowly and fully, and breathe out slowly and fully. Let go of any expectations. Just sit quietly and observe your breath. If it helps, you might like to imagine a balloon, and each time you exhale, the balloon rises higher. Watch the balloon with your mind's eye as it rises slowly higher and higher, and you begin to feel calmer and calmer. As you watch the balloon, you will notice your breathing slows down. As you watch the balloon float and fly, you feel a sense of peace and quiet. As you watch the balloon, you feel your physical self relax and let go. Your mind focuses only on the breath. Nothing else matters. If you feel that your mind starts to wander, accept this without judgement of yourself and gently coax your mind back to the breath. You may want to associate a word with your inhalation and a word with your exhalation. With the inhale, you may say to yourself the word 'comfort'. With the exhale, you may say 'let go'. I like to set a time for meditation. You could start with five minutes and develop up to 20 minutes as you feel more comfortable. Choose a time which works for you.

2. **Observation**

This practice is about consciously observing an object that induces a feeling of comfort in you. For me, this is often an apple but for you it might be something else. My children, for instance, use a favourite toy for this practice. Perhaps you could use a piece of fruit or some treasured possession. Choose something simple so you can focus all your attention into your senses, observing the colour and texture of the item, becoming aware of its taste or its scent, listening to how it sounds when you touch or tap it. Notice how it feels beneath your fingers and what it means to you, without letting your mind rush into the future.

If you have chosen something edible like a piece of fruit, you may wish to just touch it or you might like to eat it too. I often use pieces of fruit as a trigger for this exercise because they have such interesting textures and we often forget how great they can taste. This is what I do. I sit down with my beautiful wooden chopping block in front of me. (This chopping block also holds special significance for me.) I pick up an apple. I smell the apple and run my fingers over its skin to feel its texture. Perhaps I might tap that apple to hear how it sounds. I then lay the apple on the chopping block and very, very slowly cut into it as I focus on my breath. I keep my attention on my breath to keep myself in the present. If I notice my breath becomes short, it is often because I am distracted by other things or have allowed my mind to wander.

As I slide the knife into the apple, I notice its shape, its texture, its sound, its scent. I then eat the apple, enjoying its juicy crispness. The key here is that everything I do is very slow. I continue to watch my breath and be in the experience. When I finish, I say to myself "I am grateful for this moment and now I choose to finish this experience." I believe it is very important that all rituals, like this one of observation, have a deliberate opening and closing so we can choose where our thoughts are directed and when to stop our practice. You can try the same approach with your object. Just spend some time observing it intently. Keep your attention on your breath and senses. Take time with this ritual. Don't rush. What do you notice? What do you feel? The gift of this experience is to find peace in the process and to focus on the moment you are in.

There are many simple experiences we do each day which help us feel good. This exercise is about learning to identify some of these things and to consider what elements of these practices enhance our lives. Instead of seeing happiness in the acquisition of an item, we can begin to recognise that it is feelings of comfort, human connection and rewarding goals which actually make us feel happy and that these come from a state of mind within. Once we identify this, we can develop our practice. This is about uncluttered simplicity, so notice how it feels to devote yourself to what you do without distraction, because it is in the distraction that the experience of happiness is lost.

What value did you find in this exercise?

My response (meditation): I noticed that when I focused upon the simple act of breathing, my mind immediately started to calm and be in the present. As I developed the ability to stay with the breath, I felt at first stillness and peace, but with time this became awareness, and eventually compassion. I felt grounded and content. The more I practiced, the more I felt self-aware, and the more contented I felt. I particularly noticed that this has a gradual cumulative effect.

Your response:

_____
_____
_____
_____

My response (observation exercise): *I noticed that when I sat in the simplicity of an act such as eating an apple, I was aware of senses such as touch, smell, texture and taste, and my enjoyment of the experience increased significantly. It was as if I could magnify my feelings with focus and practice. I realised with these simple exercises that happiness is indeed a practice and a skill which may improve with repetition, but only if I made the decision to do so and put in the practice.*

Your response:

_____
_____
_____
_____

What did you learn from these exercises?

My response: *With both of these exercises, I learned that happiness is a skill that requires application, repetition and devotion. I was actually surprised with how my ability to notice, observe and feel self-aware progressively increased with practice. I also learned that these simple exercises helped me to feel relaxed and at peace for the rest of the day. I found that*

CHAPTER 1

the focus upon repetition was almost like rocking myself into a state of calm.

Your response:
_____
_____
_____
_____

The three ways we feel happiness

In the days following the end of my marriage, I literally felt like I could not move. My chest was tight, I felt nauseous, and my mind was foggy. It was as if my body were shutting down. I spent several days in bed, hiding under the doona for hours at a time, hoping that life outside would miraculously go back to the way it was. Of course it didn't. Instead, I had to learn how to move forward into the new reality of my world. It took about four years for me to really just start to cope. I struggled with the changes in my friendship groups, my location and my business, as well as the loss of so many familiar habits and rituals. With time (and I do mean *lots* of time), I realised that change is inevitable but that happiness is a choice. It is also, I discovered, a responsibility.

As the preceding exercise has shown, part of developing our ability to feel happiness involves becoming more aware of how we may experience and practice it. But as we are also beginning to see, happiness can be found in simple, daily activities. I believe there are three interacting ways through which we can feel happiness and that each of these is important to our overall wellbeing. It is my view that we cannot be happy without experiencing all three types of happiness in balance and these are brought together through the meaning we choose to give our lives. What meaning do you give your life? And what behaviours do you have that reflect this meaning?

Ways of feeling happy

1. Comfort – A feeling of cosy pleasure, calm or quiet enjoyment experienced through the senses. I am not talking about a euphoric high here, but rather the comfort brought on through the experience of simple acts, such as drinking a hot mug of soup, resting on a downy pillow, sliding your feet into soft slippers, getting swept away by wonderful music, or sharing a heartfelt hug.

2. Empathetic engagement – The deep satisfaction brought on by giving and receiving empathy in relationships, by demonstrating care and love, and engaging in listening and conversation. This is a kind of connection between people that is displayed not just in words but also in actions. I am big on actions. It is easy to say words but the practice of these words is where the truth lies.

3. Rewarding goals – The sense of enjoyment and fulfilment brought on not only by achieving a goal but also aspiring towards that goal (Rutledge, Skandalia, Dayanc, & Dolana, 2014). Remember, it is in the delight of the journey that happiness lies. Don't you just enjoy those precious moments when you plan with anticipation and a level of excitement towards a goal, a dream or a creation? I know I do. For example, if you have the goal of going on a holiday, then enjoy the anticipation, the planning, and the counting down of the days towards the event, as well as the event itself. Experience and sit in that anticipation. For me, planning towards, creating

and imagining the publishing of this book has brought me so much happiness. Visualise the journey towards the goal as part of the joy rather than wait until the moment that the goal is achieved.

What brings our experiences of cosy comfort, empathetic engagement and rewarding goals together is the precious meaning we choose to give our lives. This meaning drives our purpose, our contentment and our relationships. Our drive towards happiness needs to be fuelled by something that goes beyond who we are (Seligman, 2010). Often, it is by giving to the community and to others through our expressions of compassion, gratitude or empathy that we feel meaningful. Finding a balance across these different ways of feeling happiness provides us with our sense of wellbeing. We will discuss further how these three ways of feeling happy can be experienced through the practice of daily rituals and will explore the idea how our daily happy practice can instil meaning into our lives and indeed into the lives of others. For now, however, let us keep our focus on the present and reflect on how our current happiness fits into this framework.

Exercise 3: What makes you happy?

In this exercise, I want you to take a moment to think about the things that make you feel happy and add meaning to your life. Perhaps you enjoy a cup of tea in your favourite cup with the morning paper and the sun shining in through the window. Maybe you cherish the feeling of having a hot shower then drying yourself with soft, fluffy towels and getting into your favourite pyjamas or other comfortable clothing. You might enjoy a weekly meeting with a friend over wine and cards or a brisk walk with the dog when you can feel the crisp twilight air against your face. Do you feel happiness when you say grace at the dinner table or have a weekly date night with your partner? What does date night involve for you? Candles? Music? A favourite meal? What about at birthdays and religious or cultural ceremonies? Do you have a fitness routine you enjoy, or a special way of celebrating your friendships?

Using the table below, list all the activities you can think of which bring you happiness. Remember, these are things that you already do. We are just trying to draw your attention to these experiences. Once you have your list, note down next to each item the way in which it makes you feel happy. Do you enjoy a physical sensation of comfort? Is it the pleasure of making a meaningful connection? Or do you cherish the feeling of celebration or reward? It is ok if you feel more than one type of happiness for an individual activity. For instance, giving a friend a hug could make you feel happy due to feelings of both comfort and empathetic connection, and a hug can be pretty rewarding too. Making sure your room is neat and tidy could generate for you a sense of reward and also of comfort.

Take some time and write down as many activities as you can think of that currently bring you happiness. I have included some from my own life to give you an example of how to complete the table. Remember that your happy activity may relate to just one of the categories or perhaps to all three. It is not about the category itself. Rather, it is about noticing ordinary activities which help you feel happy and consciously practicing these.

Happy activity or experience (Any activity or experience you enjoy)	Comforting (Feelings of comfort, calm or quiet pleasure)	Empathetic engagement (Feelings of empathy, engagement and social connection)	Rewarding (Feelings of anticipation of reward, achievement and celebration)
Drinking tea	I feel a sense of calm when sipping my favourite English breakfast tea in my favourite china cup in my soft, comfy meditation chair		
Going for a walk	I enjoy the feeling of going for a walk along the local bush trails, listening to the birds as the sun sets.		
Meeting my friend Anita for a glass of wine		I enjoy listening to Anita, sharing eye contact with her, and engaging in the personal, caring nature of our conversation. I also appreciate how Anita listens without making any judgment.	I look forward to meeting Anita and think about what we will chat about with anticipation. I consider the meaning of our friendship, what it adds to my life and how it inspires me. Afterwards, I reflect upon how pleasant it was to spend time with Anita.
Creating my podcast 'Being Well with Lauren'		As I record each podcast, I feel like I am sitting and having a cup of tea with friends, so the virtual experience of engaging is enjoyable. I feel a sense of connection with my listeners through each upload of a show.	I look forward to recording each podcast and find the experience of loading the podcasts and receiving comments most rewarding. I feel a sense of achievement each time. It is not just the creating of each episode, it is also the drinking of tea as I record the podcast, the listening to the show as I edit, and the anticipation of comments from my friends after it has loaded.

What value did you find in this exercise?

My response: *I find this exercise is valuable because it helps me identify the practices and routine behaviours which enhance my life. It also allows me to focus on the aspects of these practices that add to my life. Instead of seeing happiness in the acquisition of an item, I am able to recognise that it is found in comfort, human connection and meaningful reward, in the ordinary activities of each day.*

Your response:

_____
_____
_____
_____

What did you learn from this exercise?

My response: *I learned to identify the potential for happiness in simple, anticipated and ordinary day to day activities. Doing this exercise made me realise that happiness is all around me. I just have to choose to experience it.*

Your response:

_____
_____
_____
_____

CHAPTER 1

One of my favourite rituals for happiness

How are you going so far, my friends? You have already learned what happiness means to you, have practiced the art of noticing and have considered some different ways you experience happiness. Now it is time for us to begin exploring how rituals can help us feel happy every day. I explained in the introduction to this book what rituals are and why they matter. Now I want to describe to you one of my favourite rituals. This is something I love to do and it can be a really valuable part of your journey too. It allows me to pause, observe, reflect and learn. It teaches me about myself, and my children enjoy doing it too. This ritual is journaling and it is part of a larger ritual that brings daily happiness to my family.

Life with four kids is incredibly hectic and I often feel that I am riding by the seat of my pants. I find it is really important for us to regularly stop and meet as a family to discuss our processes and remind ourselves of our values. That's why every day, no matter what, we all sit down to dinner together without any outside distraction. This one ritual forms the backbone of our closeness. Like all our rituals, it occurs at a particular time, in a particular sequence and at a particular place. In order for rituals to help mould our minds, it is essential that they are habitual and have a defined structure.

There are several components to our family dinners, each of which helps us to come together, communicate with each other, and feel happy. One of the most treasured parts for me is our journaling practice. After dinner is finished and we have washed the dishes and wiped down the table, we get out our journals and sit down once more. Each of us has our own journal, always kept in the same place.

Sitting around the dinner table, without music or iPhones or any other distractions, we each do ten minutes of journaling.

As my children are aged between nine and thirteen, I only expect them to write around half a page to a page of words. There are four principal components or prompts in our journaling. We write about:
- our daily experiences
- our feelings of gratitude
- our reflections and learnings
- our goals.

After we complete our journal writing, we generally read what we have written out to the whole family. My children really enjoy this part. This helps them notice particular moments, feel a sense of being heard and be grateful for their day. It also helps us as family members to get a feeling for each other's experiences and to develop empathy. Sharing our journaling like this is not about providing solutions or making judgments. It is just listening. In this way, I also learn more about my children's days and it gives us precious time to be with each other.

The kids have made the decision to add drawings, quotes and other resources into their diary. There is a resilience component happening here as well. By reading out the events of their days, my children learn to develop perseverance and perspective. They become the observer of the event rather than the experiencer of it. I am often surprised by what they read out and find myself thinking, "Wow, I didn't realise that she felt that" or "I'm so impressed he achieved that" or "I wasn't aware they suffered or learned in that way."

Through our daily journaling practice, we feel the joy of reflection, sharing and learning. It is such a simple practice, but it has amazing results, as this story illustrates. Each Saturday, my boys play domestic and representative level basketball.

CHAPTER 1

They are very serious about their sport and have clear goals they want to achieve. Every morning, they rise at 6.30 a.m. and practice their skills. (This is their idea, by the way, not mine.) They practice again after school. A few weeks back, my son Max scored eleven points in his game and my son Seth scored six.

A few days later, they both wrote about their goals for basketball in their journals. They wrote about what practice drills they would do and how many points they would score on the weekend. They also wrote about how they would feel. Max wrote that he intended to score four points and Seth wrote a motivational phrase, saying he will 'never give up'. The next Saturday, Max said to me after the game, "Mum, that journal is like magic. When I believe in myself, magic happens." Being a proud mum, I hugged him and didn't say anything, but speaking personally, I don't think journal writing is magic. Rather, it is an essential tool which equips my children and me with a method to document our feelings, observe our self-talk, and nurture our belief in ourselves. It is a tool that you can use too.

The practice of daily journaling

A vital part of understanding who and where we are today lies in our ability to lay our cards on the table, observe our actions, review our thoughts and learn from what we discover. This is where journaling is so valuable. I have found so many benefits in the practice of journaling and I want you to experience them too. Throughout the chapters of this book, I will be giving you lots of prompts to write in your journal, so let's start right away. Here is what I want you to do. Get yourself a pen and a book with blank pages and begin where you are right now with your own journal. Start by writing down where you are and how you are feeling. You might wish to make a note about the time of day or what the weather is like. Then I want you to write just one or two lines about what you have learned so far by reading this book. Think about the exercises you have done and how they made you feel. What have they revealed to you? Have you enjoyed doing them? Have you wondered at the point of them? Perhaps you might like to write about what it feels like to be starting this journey towards becoming happier. Are you nervous, excited, encouraged, optimistic?

Once you've made a start with your journal, I invite you to treat it like a friend or someone you can confide in. Use it to record your thoughts and insights as you read through this book. Then, once you feel comfortable recording your thoughts and impressions, make a commitment to yourself to write in your journal every day. You might decide, like my family, to write at the same time every day. Another option is to write for the same amount of time each day, by setting a timer for a specified duration and writing until the timer goes off. The point is to develop a practice you can stick to. If you are not sure what to write about, you could use the same prompts as my family do in our journaling practice. Here they are again, with a bit more detail this time.

- Daily experiences – Write a brief description of the events of your day. What really stood out to you? What made you happy? What did you pay attention to? What do you want to remember about this day?
- Gratitude – Think about the things you are grateful for today. Write down as many of these as you can. They can be big things or small ones.
- Reflection, review and learning – What did you discover about yourself today? What could you have done differently? How will you approach tomorrow based on what you have learned today?
- Goals – What do you want to have happen in your life?

> What goals do you hold and what do you need to do each day to achieve these? What progress have you made today? (Remember that although it is good to set these goals, it is the journey which is important here.)

It may take you a little while to get used to the practice of writing in your journal every day, so be gentle with yourself. I am sure that as soon as you start to see the benefits of journaling, you will come to enjoy it as much as I do. You can think of journaling as a kind of journey in itself. In fact, it incorporates the other essential concepts of this book too. It allows us to become more aware of our way of seeing, it helps us with the art of noticing, it enables us to reflect, and it is a practice we can commit to doing. This leads me to the final, important point I want to make in this chapter, which is about your decision to make a commitment to your own happiness.

Making a commitment to your happiness

Remember my six beliefs about happiness that I outlined in the introduction? One of those is that happiness requires a conscious decision and intentional action, while another says that happiness takes skill and practice. We often fear making changes in our lives and sometimes we do not hold ourselves accountable to our word. But I believe our ability to make a decision and stay true to it adds meaning to our lives and defines who we are. A friend of mine, Bruce Davis, used to say that responsibility is the 'ability to respond'. I love that phrase, as it really indicates that being responsible means having the ability to act on our decisions in response to our values and to make stuff happen, and a big part of our happiness comes from making a decision to be happy.

As Aristotle says, "Happiness depends upon ourselves." This means that happiness can only be realised when we take responsibility for ourselves and take action in support of our decisions. This requires making a commitment to our own happiness. A commitment implies devoting ourselves to a cause. It is usually based on our values and beliefs, and requires making a series of ongoing decisions, rather than one isolated one. That takes practice and dedication. If you are serious about feeling happy every day of your life, then I encourage you to make that commitment to yourself. If you are prepared to do this, then there is just one more thing I would like you to do before we continue on our journey. I'm excited because this will also be your first ritual.

Are you ready?

Your first ritual: Happiness practice contract

You know from the previous section on journaling how I feel about putting pen to paper. Writing something down means that we must think about what we are saying. When we write out our commitments and place them somewhere visible, we can look at our own words, reflect on them and remind ourselves of why they matter to us. That is why I want you now to get out your pen, open your journal and write out a happy practice contract for yourself like the one I use (below). I have this contract on the wall in my bathroom so I can look at it when I am preparing for my day or winding down in the evening. I use it to remind myself of the decision I have made to be responsible for my own happiness.

You may wish to change some of the wording to make it your own, but I suggest you write something like this:

Chapter 1

My commitment to my daily happiness

I, Lauren Ostrowski Fenton, decide to be happy every day. I will focus upon exploring the moments of happiness presented to me in each day. I will train my mind to see, feel and act with positivity, realistic optimism and compassion.

I accept that there are some things I cannot change, but I will work with resilience and optimism on the things I can change. I take responsibility for my own happiness and I commit to being happy.

I also commit to completing my happiness practice daily. I accept that some days it may be harder than others to feel happy. On these days, I will accept my practice as it is and accept myself as I am.

I will feel the happy moments in each day and I will feel grateful for these moments.

Signature

Date

Doesn't it feel good to make that commitment to yourself? The words *I will*, *I take responsibility* and *I commit* are important here because they are about personal belief and taking action in the present. Once you have decided on the wording of your happiness practice contract, find somewhere special to keep it. You may wish to print it out and place somewhere you will see it often or you might prefer to keep it more private. Wherever you decide to put it, make it a ritual to read and reflect upon it every single day. You might like to meditate on it, recite it aloud or repeat it to yourself before you go to sleep. The more dedicated you are to enhancing your own happiness, the more you will find yourself able to feel happy.

In a nutshell

Well, my friends, we have reached the end of the first chapter. How are you feeling? Keep trying to observe your feelings and your self-talk, but don't expect too much of yourself yet. Remember, the art of noticing is a skill that you will develop over time. Use your journal to make some notes about what you have learned and how you are doing so far. To assist you with your reflections, here is a quick list of the main ideas we have been discussing:

- Happiness is a state of present experience. In order to feel happy, you need to begin where you are.
- There are many different definitions of happiness and the 'easy' approach to happiness is not always the most sustainable one.
- No one can hand us the answer to our happiness because we are the only ones who can make ourselves happy.
- We all have current beliefs and experiences of happiness, and it is a good idea to become aware of these.
- Set point theory proposes to us that around 50% of our happiness is predetermined, leaving us with up to 50% to play with.
- We can learn to notice our happiness through practices like meditation and observation.
- The three ways we can feel happiness are comfort, engagement and reward, and we can think about our current experiences of happiness in these three ways.

Chapter 1

- Rituals can help us feel happy every day.
- Journaling is a powerful tool that can help us document our feelings, observe our self-talk, and nurture our belief in ourselves, especially if we do it every day.
- Happiness involves making a commitment, taking intentional action, and developing a practice that reinforces the meaning in our lives.

In the next chapter, we will take another significant step on our journey. We will learn the importance of understanding ourselves and why self-acceptance is essential for happiness. I will also share more of my own story, including some parts of it that I have never told anyone before.

Chapter 2
SELF-AWARENESS IS THE KEY TO HAPPINESS

DO YOU FEEL good about yourself? Do you believe you are good enough? Take a moment to think about it. Do you like who you are? Do you feel comfortable being you? Are you able to see your strengths and weaknesses clearly and objectively? Can you embrace your whole self, including all those funny habits and personality quirks? When you reflect on your life, does your recollection of your experiences support or diminish your sense of self and wellbeing? Do you trust yourself and your own opinions? Do you accept yourself?

Some of you may be feeling uncomfortable with these questions or perhaps you might find them overwhelming. If that is how you feel, I understand. It is hard to take a good hard look at yourself, isn't it? I know that I found it hard. It's so much easier to rationalise our present position in order to remain within our comfort zone. I once wanted to see myself as the helpless victim of yesterday, whereas being happy is really about taking responsibility for today. Happiness is about asking the hard questions and it all starts with self-awareness. I say to my children that if happiness were a house, then our self-awareness would be the concrete foundations and our values and beliefs would be the framework. Our happiness is built upon these foundations and this framework.

Crisp and Turner (2010, p. 2) define self-awareness as "a psychological state in which people are aware of their traits, feelings and behaviour." Self-awareness is really just about being able to have that good hard look at ourselves, to have perspective, recognise that we are capable of change, and have the courage to be who we are. And yes, in my journey, I found that being myself took real courage. Self-awareness is also about being able to let go of the need to be found right and refusing to be defined by the opinion of others. To be aware of your fears, your feelings and your thoughts and then to channel this awareness in a direction which brings you happiness, well, that is the key.

The best thing we can do for ourselves is to get in touch with what we feel, what we believe and what motivates us. How do we do this? How do we become more self-aware in order to experience happiness consistently? It starts with what we say to ourselves. Yes, that's right. We must begin by exploring our self-talk with honesty. Even though you may not know it, we all practice self-talk. It is that inner voice which works like a running commentary, telling our subconscious who we are and noticing then internalising each experience. A self-aware person uses self-talk which is self-accepting but simultaneously open to change, such as:

- I accept my limitations but I work towards self-improvement
- I like the company of friends but I know how to enjoy my own company
- I feel comfortable in my own skin but I am willing to explore opportunities for change

- At times I may feel fear, anxiety or doubt, but I am prepared to address these feelings
- I work towards resolution and change where possible and accept or withdraw from situations where necessary.

Do you say these sort of things to yourself? Are you self-aware, self-accepting and self-assertive? Or is your self-talk a little more doubtful, rationalising, and lacking in self worth? Developing self-awareness is a great way to learn more about yourself and enhance your self-acceptance and understanding, but it only comes when we can truly look in the mirror at the reflection of who we are as individuals. Being self-aware is not easy. It takes practice. I remember the first time I tried this, I looked in the mirror and only saw what others told me. I saw a victim who felt resentment and self doubt. I saw someone who needed reassurance and liked to please others without having any defined boundaries. It took time and practice to look past my hurt to the person I ultimately am. And it will take you time, so take that time and be kind to yourself.

You may be thinking that you are not capable of self-awareness. Perhaps you feel too hurt or lost to feel self-understanding, or maybe you imagine you are not worthy of self-acceptance. If you believe this, you are not alone. I hear you. I once held those ideas about myself. Sometimes when we have a hurtful experience, we can allow it to define us, to define our feelings and thoughts and the present moment. Well, that was me. To be honest, I have felt a lack of self-acceptance since early childhood. There is nothing like the imprint of an unhappy memory to affect our perception of ourselves. Maybe, like me, you had an experience of bullying, judgement or exclusion which you have carried throughout your youth

CHAPTER 2

into adulthood. But one key concept that I have found essential to letting go of a past hurt is self-awareness.

To be fully self-aware, we need to accept ourselves for who we are and take responsibility for our actions. We need to learn from, review and develop through these actions. With understanding comes an awareness of the reality of any situation, while acceptance allows us to detach from expecting or needing a particular outcome. I want to be clear here on what I mean by acceptance. Acceptance is not about apathy. Acceptance is about a quiet, resilient knowledge of your limitations and weaknesses without any reactivity and with a genuine willingness to work through these limitations honestly and assertively in order to grow in wisdom and self-knowledge. When we have self-acceptance, we are no longer affected by the judgment of others, and nor do we constantly need their approval. We can let go of unrealistic expectations of ourselves and just enjoy being who we truly are. That's what this chapter is all about.

To help you understand how important this is, I want to share some of my personal history. I should warn you that this is not a bedtime story, although it does ultimately have a happy ending. What I want you to know is that our minds absorb our stories and shape themselves accordingly. People don't force our perceptions upon us; we do that ourselves. We choose how we see our world and that means our story is the one we choose to write. It has taken me close to fifty years to understand this. I want you to benefit from my experiences, so let's take a journey back in time. Let us explore my story and how it has changed my way of seeing and my self-acceptance.

I am a toddler. I am the older of two children with four more siblings yet to come. I speak both Polish and English. I can walk, but it is a bit like a penguin shuffle, with my little hands stretched out in front of me for balance. I utter a word or perhaps make a sound as I take uncertain steps into our lounge room. My father is sitting on the couch. He hears me and quickly swings around. His face is full of big smiling teeth. He sweeps me up into a bear hug, calling me 'Biggie'. Everything I say and do elicits gestures of love and pride from him. I hear him exaggerate my strengths to others. He describes me as one would describe a superhero. According to my father, I eat a kilogram of steak per day, run like the wind and am incredibly smart.

I am aged four. I remember running to the garage to greet my father when he arrived home from work each night. "*Tatuś*," I would call out to him in Polish. I remember the love in his welcoming face and his exuberance. I remember feeling that I was the centre of his world. There was one particularly meaningful occasion when I ran up to my dad at Melbourne airport when he arrived home from a visit to Poland. This memory stands out in my mind purely and simply because of the love I remember seeing etched on Dad's face.

At home, my mother teaches me letters and words from cards with hand drawn pictures. I remember a picture of a big, round cat with a long, wavy tail and buttons running down its chest. Every time I get a word right, she smiles with love. If I get the word wrong, she encourages me patiently. I am told that I am loved and that I am clever. I remember being toilet trained because my mum sat by me for long periods of time, reading to me in Polish and English. These memories give me a profound sense of worth. I remember her warm smiles when I got the words right and I remember her gentle, patient encouragement. I recall my mother coming back from a trip to Poland and falling asleep on my bed. I lie really still, squashed up

CHAPTER 2

against the wall, trying to hold my breath so I don't wake her. I watch her face as she sleeps. Her lips are slightly parted. I enjoy her motherly scent and the sound of her breathing.

I remember Christmas gatherings around the tree and the sound of Polish carols being sung. My dad loves these carols. He can't hold a note but that doesn't matter. There is the enjoyment of taking turns in opening our presents and our happy, dancing eyes as the wrapping paper falls upon the floor. There is so much wrapping paper! I feel like I could swim through it. I run through the paper and it makes a rustling sound that I like. I feel a strong sense of family. We eat traditional Polish food at our Christmas meals. My father is really excited and my mother tries to calm him down. He is laughing and talking a little too loudly. There is so much food upon the table. My father eats too much.

These are good memories. But for some reason, I do not allow them to significantly shape the way I see my world. Perhaps this is because I am the eldest and do not have an older sibling to follow. Perhaps it is because I am the What If Girl, already worrying about what could go wrong. Whatever the reason, I find that over time, these memories recede and others take over instead. But writing this book brings these joyful memories back to me.

I am six years old. I am sitting at a wooden desk towards the back of the classroom. There are no computers here, just grey lead pencils and rough paper resting upon wooden desks. The room feels cold and sounds echo through it. I lean forward at my desk, trying to listen to the teacher. I attempt to separate the sound of her voice from the other sounds in the room. At times I find the noise confusing. There is the sound of a chair scraping across the polished floorboards and a pencil scratching on paper at the next desk. I hear the sound of a page turning and a conversation directly behind me. All of these sounds are loud to me. I don't know which sound to tune in to. I struggle to learn.

I feel stressed by these many sounds. My mind struggles to focus on what the teacher is saying. I find myself tapping my fingers against each other in a deliberate, rhythmic pattern which becomes faster and faster. The fluorescent light above me seems too bright and the flickering is almost like an abrasive stroke against my skin. It is hard for me to focus with the flickering of the light. It bothers me. I turn to my left and read the titles on the spines of books in the bookcase, wondering about the stories contained within each. The windows behind the shelves take up most of the wall. I look out to a tall row of conifers. The trees sway in the wind and are full of magpies and sparrows. I watch the swaying of the branches and imagine the sound of the wind whistling. Left to right, then right to left, then back again they sway. I imagine they might be speaking to me and dancing with each other – a waltz perhaps? I feel myself swaying and then I notice the girl sitting next to me is staring at me. I sense her disapproval.

The teacher is speaking. Although I try, I can't seem to hear her. It is not that she is not speaking loudly enough, but rather that to me it seems like she is speaking from underwater. I am distracted by the sounds, sights and happenings all around me. It is like being caught in the middle of a major highway with cars racing all around. I switch back and forth, not knowing where to look, what to focus upon and what to listen to. The sounds create pictures in my mind. I start automatically to create stories from the images. It is like a movie unfolding in my head, almost beyond my control. All it takes is one sight, one sound, one scent to trigger my mind into creating and editing its own movie, complete with characters, setting

Chapter 2

and plot. My mind has left the classroom now and is travelling into an imaginary story.

Once I start imagining a story, my whole focus goes into the story and nothing else exists. I might look outside and the classroom becomes a tug boat, sailing on a windy sea with white-tipped waves slapping at its sides. At times, the teacher is a fire-breathing dragon and her coloured nails become sharp talons and the desks become castles and the students are knights and mythical creatures. I look down and feel the dizziness of vertigo as I peer down at the moat all around me. These images and stories take over my mind. I am now in my story and no longer in the classroom. I see, hear, taste and feel the story in my mind, and then suddenly I hear the teacher addressing the class in a stern voice, telling us to continue with an exercise the instructions for which I had not heard. With some trepidation I ask the teacher to please repeat herself. She frowns and says dismissively, "You never listen, Lauren. I won't help you." I see her lack of understanding as disapproval, and view my own inability to focus on one sound as stupidity. I call myself stupid. I know I am different and I don't like it. I yearn to be like the other students. At times through the year, this teacher tells me I am mentally slow or retarded. I believe her. I stop talking in class. I stop asking questions. I stop feeling comfortable about myself.

On one occasion when I don't respond to a question, the teacher drags me up by my hair. I have long blond plaits so they are easy to pull. She yanks me up on them sharply. I feel fear, so much fear. I feel a bad sensation in my stomach, like something is terribly wrong but I am not sure what it is. I don't understand why she is hurting me. I blame myself. I don't answer her, as I fear her. I don't speak at school. One day, she places her hands around my throat and squeezes. I still refuse to speak to her. She believes my decision to stop speaking is deliberate insolence. I am silent in class for a long time, perhaps several months. I stopped speaking because I saw no purpose in speaking. The children call me names like 'retard', 'psycho' and 'slow'.

The teacher takes me to the headmaster. I am really scared and feel sick inside. I remember feeling this sick sensation through a lot of my childhood. The headmaster stands up and leans forward, spitting into my face with ferocity. He tells me to listen. I am only six. I don't answer but I look up at him. Instead of listening to what he is saying, I watch his bulbous, rolling, watery eyes. In my imaginative mind, I am taken to a place where a terrifying mythical monster has round, rolling, watery eyes and I imagine the birds outside are my allies in this place. I can't hear the headmaster any more. I am inside my story. Angry, the headmaster and my teacher discuss my 'problems' in front of me. I believe what they say about me. I do not have the life experience to see that they lack insight. I allow this experience in the classroom with this damaged, abusive, violent teacher to shape my life and affect my way of seeing my world. At the age of six, I make her right and myself wrong. At the age of six, I realise that I am different and I believe that makes me wrong.

I am now aged seven. At school, I feel that I am not good enough. I am not sure how to relate to the other school children because I feel I am different from them. I play a lot of imaginary games. In sport, we play poison ball. I lack hand-eye coordination and struggle to throw a ball with any level of dexterity. I ask not to play. It takes courage for me to ask. The teacher makes me play anyway. I stand in the middle of the court with children all around me. I cannot see the ball coming, as there are so many sights and sounds. The children are laughing and screaming at me. I cannot concentrate.

Chapter 2

I am scared. The children hit me with the ball and laugh. Their laughter is loud. I feel fear. Someone calls me stupid. I tell myself the other children are right. I feel clumsy. I stand still and look down at my feet. The teacher does not understand why I stop speaking. The other pupils call me Mr Magoo, the name of a cartoon character who is a near-sighted, clumsy and uncoordinated old man. The name sticks with me throughout primary school.

The other children are often mean. One day two boys approach me. I wonder if they are going to play with me. They walk me away from the group and force me to sit on dog faeces. They laugh and walk away, leaving me there sitting on the dog faeces. They are laughing. I am called names. 'Weird', 'retard', 'slow', 'psycho', 'unco', and others. I don't remember learning much in school but I do remember feeling very scared. I felt so scared that I was nauseous. I had a dark and very bad feeling in my stomach. Looking back, I think it was dread. I remember today the sight of other children's shoes, as I was always looking down. I remember the smell of the classroom and the sounds within it. I don't remember learning anything. Instead, I allow the names given to me by others to define my sense of self. Instead of seeing my ability to create stories as a gift, I see it as a curse. I let this experience shape my life.

I am aged ten. Up until grade six, the lack of support given to me from my teachers affects the other children and so they tease me, exclude me and bully me. I eat my lunch away from them, which only further alienates me. I struggle to fit in. I want to make friends but I am not quite sure what to say. I lack the confidence to interact with others and prefer to imagine my ideas and stories by myself. There are many occasions of bullying and cruelty. In class, I notice that the other kids can not read as easily as I do. The book boxes at school are marked by reading level. I take note of the level the popular kids are at and make sure I do not progress beyond them. I hide my ability to read so that I am not further earmarked as different. .

I can write well too. I keep journals and exercise books full of my stories, which I hide. I write about animals and people in families. I write about grief, love and friendship. I do not show my stories to my teachers as I notice that the other children do not write as fluently as I can. I want to be the same as them. That is why I pretend I can't read. I don't remember being taught anything in primary school until I reach grade six when my teacher is dear Mr Savage. He tells me I am an extraordinary writer with an amazing imagination and he marks all my essays as A++++, with a multitude of pluses in red pen. I begin to wonder if I am not actually a 'retard', but instead a reasonable writer as Mr Savage believes I am. Mr Savage had a profound effect upon my life. I start to write more.

I am aged twelve. One day at school, the sports teacher makes us run a one kilometre block. Although the run is hard, I notice that I can do it. There are no balls to watch and no agility required, just running. It makes me feel good and clears my mind, helping me to focus. I am equal first in the school's literature prize with the smartest girl in class for a story I wrote about a baby kangaroo who loses his mother to hunters. (My father keeps that story to this day.) I start to exercise and it becomes a habit. I notice that the more I exercise, the more I can focus my mind. Every day I get off the bus early and run home across the hills. I find that I can think more clearly when I exercise and so exercise becomes a big part of my life. I realise I like order and structure, and exercise gives this to me. I want more exercise. Later in life, I become an aerobics teacher, a gym instructor and a personal trainer. I run. I cycle. I swim and I kayak. My love of exercise becomes self-defining. I lecture in fitness and motivation for a number of institutions. I compete in triathlons, ultra-marathons and natural body building competitions. Exercise helps quieten my mind and contributes significantly to my happiness.

I am aged thirty-five. As I grow older, I begin to see that my way of thinking is very different from other people's. I realise that I think in sequential pictures, like a film. The only way I can explain it is that I see the whole film almost at once. It just unfolds like dominoes as soon as I have a trigger experience with sight, sound or smell. I come up with ideas and can map out in my mind their various consequences. Clear thinking exercises are logical to me in a way that seems different to everyone else. In the workplace, I find there are some things I am exceptionally good at. I can redesign contracts and write tender proposals efficiently and effectively. I am able to analyse legal contracts quickly and can see faults in conceptual writing that others do not. Time does not exist to me when I have an idea. My colleagues seem to think differently to me and have different interests. Employers like me but other staff at times did not. In three jobs, colleagues complain to my manager that I work too fast, don't take breaks and change too many systems. They find this stressful and call me weird. I try to slow down to fit in and please them. Someone tells me, "You think much faster than everyone else and people don't understand that. You're just weird."

I struggle at times in some of my relationships with other adults. I lack boundaries to protect myself and I want them to approve of me. I try to be like them so they will include me. I am still not married and do not have children. I feel a little lost at family gatherings, as I am different from my siblings, who are happily married with children. I am worried that I am growing older and feel my biological clock ticking. I still need a lot of time and space to myself. More than others, it seems. Often, I feel a sense of failure. It is not until I learn to stop needing approval and caring about being seen as different that I start to accept who I am. With acceptance comes understanding and I start to feel ok about myself. My perceived weaknesses as a child become my strengths as an adult. I worry less about how others see my differences. If they can not love me for who I am, then I decide that is their problem, not mine. I start to understand that each of us is different and that is ok. But I still struggle with a sense of self. I still want to be like others.

I am aged forty-four. I have four children. I am married to a man who is a landscape gardener and has a gerbera farm. He is a big man with a contagious laugh who tells entertaining stories around the dinner table, gesticulating enthusiastically with his hands. He has a gift with plants. He creates gardens for me as gifts. They are beautiful. I have a stone garden, a secret garden and other gardens. He also plants surprises for me as well. He plants bright yellow daffodils everywhere, scattered with love. When the bulbs blossom, it is as if our garden is full of bright jewels. I love these daffodils. He surprises me by planting a mature weeping cherry tree right outside our bedroom window. It is just for me. We live on a 12 acre farm and I run a wellbeing centre. We are close to the local beach and often take long walks on it. I love the sunsets. There is a row of pine trees which stand tall at the front of our garden. As the sun sets, they sometimes sway in the breeze. We have a pet cow called Talulabelle and a Great Dane called Charlie. I love our life. But having four kids, including twins, in four years is tough. Sometimes I still need to please others to my own detriment. But my sense of my self is developing. I am not sure who I am, but I am getting there.

Chapter 2

I am aged forty-six. My marriage has ended. I have four children under the age of eight. I still feel the need to please others without having any clear boundaries around this. Now my label of 'married mother' has been taken away. I feel very different again. I feel that I have failed. I am alone and lacking in self-acceptance, but I now have the unfamiliar and daunting label of 'divorced and single mother'. I am very sad and very lost. I decide to change and discover that changing is both hard and painful. I find YouTube and create my own channel. Through it, I meet like-minded people. It is only at the age of forty-six that I stop allowing childhood influences like that bullying teacher and my lack of dexterity to shape my sense of self. I begin to shape myself. I reflect on my life. I review and learn to accept with time. Much time. I could wish that it didn't take me so long to do this, but such regrets would be wasted. I create myself now and that is all that really counts. I understand that it takes time for me to accept myself because I was so easily affected by the judgment of others and so sensitive about how different I was. I can now appreciate that we each have gifts which make us unique and valuable.

I am aged fifty-one. I have four beautiful children who live with me most of the time. We laugh a lot. We share stories. My children love me. I am fit and healthy. I sleep fairly well. I walk and lift weights every day. I enjoy this immensely. My parents love me and care about me. I love them both so much too. I have great friends who would drop everything to help me. I cherish my daily cup of tea. The evening meal I share with my children is the highlight of my day. I have really enjoyed and grown through my experience of YouTube. I say what I think. I love my dogs. I love to hear about my children's days. I am not lonely – most of the time. I have very little money and often go without. I appreciate each day. I make mistakes and I generally own and review these mistakes. I have great memories. I have hope and goals. I love my home. I feel comfort every day. Sometimes I cry but I never give up and I can quickly find something to smile about. I don't care what others think of me most of the time. I believe in myself. I accept myself. I am proud to be different. I am happy every day.

Self understanding and happiness

These stories clearly indicate how I allowed my life to be shaped by others rather than making decisions for myself. I thought for a long time before deciding to include them in this book. There are other stories I wrote down but then later took out because they are too upsetting. It is not that I mind sharing such stories, but I feel they are too graphic and abusive for this book. You can see that I had a different way of learning than some others. I have chosen to leave out some details about this. My desire is not to sadden you with my experiences. Instead, I want to let those of you who have been bullied know that you are not alone. I want to also share with you that if you worry about what others say about you, you will become their words.

I recently posted an update on Facebook in response to a viewer's letter expressing self doubt. I wrote: *You are so much bigger than 'he said' or 'she said' but only if 'you say'. We each have infinite potential. Simply be yourself. Next time someone labels you as different, be proud … No one ever become a leader, created something new, thought of a new idea OR stepped beyond their comfort zone by being the 'same'. Resist the sheep mentality and be different and CREATE, STRIVE and ACHIEVE.* I have come a long way in order to be able say this and truly believe it. If I can do it, you can too. I want you all to know that despite whatever has happened in your life, you can still find self-acceptance and happiness.

Prior to writing this book, I had not told anyone about what happened to me at school. It was very important that I kept it secret. However, during the writing of the book, I told my parents and now I am telling you. Once I saw the stories written down on paper, they suddenly seemed so real to me. I felt so sad for little Lauren who was bullied and abused for being different and sad for all the years I wasted worrying about what others thought of me. I realised that I needed to let myself grieve. Writing has helped me with that. (Maybe it can help you too.) I tell you these stories to help explain the different ways I have seen myself and the way my self-perception has shaped my world. I tell these stories so that if you need to, you can also grieve for the little child in you.

Through choosing at times to base my self-perception on unhappy memories of people abusing me, I gave my power away to those who did not deserve it. That was a mistake. I defined myself through the labels other people gave me and wasted years feeling unworthy and unacceptable because of someone else's stories and choices. I cannot relive those years, but I can change the way I see myself now and I can share my story with you. I hope you can learn something from it. The fact that I have learned to overcome those beliefs about myself means that you can do so too, but don't think for one minute that it has been easy. It has been really tough.

I understand that I am clever, gifted and have value, but it took a long time before I could fully accept myself and start to help others. I know that you are also gifted, unique and have untapped worth, even if you can't quite see it for yourself yet. But please believe me when I tell you that self-acceptance is vital to your happiness. You can learn to accept yourself and see the beauty of who you are. Why don't you take a moment now to think about your gifts? What is special about you? What is it that really makes you who you are? You might like to spend some time writing about this in your journal.

What is important to remember is that through certain habits, practices, and yes, rituals too, we can reshape our attitudes, our beliefs and even our feelings to become more self-aware, more positive and more optimistic. We can practice the art of noticing what is really happening around us and how we are responding to particular people and situations. We can adjust our way of seeing past events and change our patterns to increase our sense of self-acceptance. It does take work, but it can be done. Like happiness itself, self-awareness is a journey that requires time, practice and resilience. Let's go through this together, step by step. Are you ready?

The three keys to self-awareness

Self-awareness has three parts. These are:

- the ability to **know yourself**, which involves insight and awareness of your core values and beliefs
- the ability to **accept yourself**, which requires kindness and the strength to see mistakes as opportunities for growth
- the ability to **develop yourself** which means building wisdom and resilience through owning your thoughts and working towards change.

These three keys are all about understanding yourself. Understanding yourself is not about arrogance or vanity. It is simply a quiet knowledge of who you are. Self-acceptance is the first crucial step here, as it involves recognising your strengths and working on your weaknesses with kindness. This is important. Every step we take in life needs to be made with kindness, both towards others and to ourselves, so please keep that in mind, my friends. Ironically, people often focus on happiness practices like gratitude, compassion and forgiveness that are directed towards others, rather than taking the time to understand and accept themselves first. How can we feel grateful for the gifts in our life if we don't see that we are a gift ourselves? How can we forgive others for their mistakes if we can not forgive ourselves? And how can we act with kindness if we do not begin by being kind to ourselves?

There is one way and one way only to self-awareness, and that starts with stillness. It is only when we are silent that we can truly hear our inner self, our consciousness, speak. The stillness I developed as an adult through meditation, prayer, self-inquiry and silence brought me self-acceptance, understanding and knowledge. Through this, I became aware of my ability to choose happiness.

1. Know yourself

Are you ready to begin your journey towards self-awareness? Are you prepared to accept yourself, know yourself and grow in wisdom? Getting to know yourself is a practice that takes a conscious effort. You do it with intention, focus and purpose. Knowing yourself means clearly identifying your values in life, your beliefs, your priorities, your moods, your habits, your physicality and your relationships. It involves understanding your strengths and weaknesses, your interests and fears, and your goals and your direction. Our social conditioning, our family, our friends, our community and our experiences all contribute to our sense of who we are and how we view the world. These values, beliefs and attitudes in turn affect our feelings, thoughts and happiness. My self-awareness has changed the way I choose to experience my life, reflect upon my life and live my life now. Consciously demonstrating our values each day is what gives us awareness of our intrinsic worth and purpose.

Values

Values are principles, standards or qualities that we hold in high regard. They reflect who we are and what matters to us. Our values help determine our priorities and our life's meaning. In a nutshell, values represent what we honour. They are very much individual and they affect us at a deep, subconscious level. If we were a boat navigating the storm of life, our values are like our rudders. Without them, we may sail forward but we have nothing to keep us on course. Every decision we make is based on our values and we use them either as avoidance, to make changes or for aspiration. It is from the springboard of our values that we choose our actions and behaviours and, indeed, our life goals.

Some of my values are:
- Family
- Fidelity
- Empathy
- Tolerance
- Forgiveness
- Integrity
- Environment
- Loyalty
- Managing my time

- Compassion
- Learning
- Wellbeing
- Finishing
- Being true to my word
- Resilience.

These values help guide the way I live my life and the decisions I make. What are some of your values? Can you identify them? Do these values support your happiness or are they at times in conflict with it? For instance, if you value your relationships but you make a decision to work 90 hours per week because you are career oriented, you may find that your priorities are not quite aligned. Or if you value your fitness but have behaviours which inhibit your health, like drinking or smoking, you are not living according to your values and you are less likely to be happy. This is why it is important to know your values and to practice the daily behaviours and habits which support these values. When we know our values, we are better able to know ourselves.

Beliefs

Our beliefs inform the way we see our world. They grow from what we see, hear, experience, read and think about, and they apply not only to how we see ourselves but also how we see other people. They are core assumptions which are so deep seated that often they go unrecognised. We tend not to question our beliefs because we think of them as being true – hence the name 'beliefs'. Many of our beliefs stem from our learning in childhood, but they may be changed or turned around later in life by 're-programming' our subconscious mind. Beliefs can be viewed in two categories as either *empowering* or *limiting.*

Empowering beliefs help us to confidently make changes in our lives. We use our empowering beliefs to make decisions in what can often be an ambiguous world. These beliefs can also lead us to create meaningful goals for ourselves and may have a communal component that enables us to care about the greater good in society. Some examples of empowering beliefs are:

- I decide how I want to feel
- I can change
- I forgive others
- I will love again
- I can say no
- I don't hold a grudge.
- I don't internalise what others think of me.

Limiting beliefs do the exact opposite of empowering beliefs and keep us rooted in particular positions. Our limiting beliefs are often based on assumptions that are not true, such as saying that you are stupid or can't learn a new language. If you spend a lot of time telling yourself that you cannot do something, then over time, this will become your reality. Some examples of limiting beliefs are:

- I can't forgive what happened to me as a child
- I will never get over my marriage ending
- I won't ever feel love again
- I am useless
- My life is hopeless.

Chapter 2

Do you have any limiting beliefs? I'd like you to take a moment to reflect upon this, as we will explore these further on in the chapter. Some examples of my own limiting beliefs are:

- I will never be able to support four kids by myself
- I will never get over my marriage ending
- I have too much baggage following the end of my marriage
- I am weird
- No one will love me again
- I am too old
- I am too scared to do this by myself

For a long time I held on to these beliefs. But with practice, I have turned these limiting beliefs into empowering ones. Today, my beliefs are:

- I am able to support four kids by myself
- I embrace the change that has arisen as a result of my marriage ending
- I am only as old as I choose to feel
- I am excited by the challenge of doing this by myself
- I enjoy my points of difference
- I know that the wisdom I will gain through this experience will bring me wonderful opportunities and lots of possibilities.

The way to change a limiting belief into an empowering one is to move away from words such as "I can't", "I won't", "I will never" and "I am not", and focus instead on phrases like "I can",

"I will", and "I am". Be careful about saying things like "I will try" or "probably", as these hold an element of doubt. Instead, make a commitment to your belief by choosing 'can do' talk and then taking action that supports it. Base these actions on your values and you will find they become even more empowering. Think for a moment if there are any words you use in your self-talk at the moment which you could change? Make a commitment to notice the words you use and consider their effect on your ability to act on your values and beliefs.

Exercise 1: Knowing your values and beliefs

This exercise is designed to help you increase your awareness of yourself. It is in two parts. The first part is about your values and the second part is about your beliefs.

Part 1: Values

What I want you to do first is to write down between five and ten values that you hold. If you are having trouble identifying your values, spend some time journaling or meditating first. Another approach you might take is to remember a time when you felt really happy. Recall that occasion in as much detail as you can. You can either write about it or just think about it. Focus your mind on what it was that made you feel so happy, then try to identify the values that are present within those features.

Once you have written down your core values, try to prioritise them. That means putting them in order of importance from one to ten. For example, for me personally, the value of 'family' is right up there at the top of my list. It helps define all the other values in my life.

CHAPTER 2

My values

1

2

3

4

5

6

7

8

9

10

When you have sorted through your list of five to ten values, spend some time reflecting on why you have chosen them. What is it about these values particularly? Where might they have they come from? Are they something you learned in childhood? Try to remember when you first began believing in each value and write down what it means to you. What is your first memory of that value? What was the trigger for that memory? I know that many of my core values come from what I learned as a child and from my loving parents. My first profound memory of my family was my dad's delight at watching me walk. Now it's your turn to think and write about what your values mean to you and why they mean that. You can do this in your journal or next to the list you have made above.

Now I want you to think about some behaviours that demonstrate your chosen values. For example if 'family' is a value you hold, you may write down behaviours like 'sit at the dinner table each night', 'hug my family', 'listen to my son read', 'develop a sleep routine', 'have a weekly movie night with popcorn' or 'play Monopoly together'. Think of at least two behaviours for each value you have listed.

Value	Behaviours
	1
	2
	1
	2
	1
	2
	1
	2
	1
	2
	1
	2
	1
	2
	1
	2
	1
	2
	1
	2

Next, think about how you might behave if others did not honour your values. How would you feel? What would you do? What boundaries might you put into place to maintain your sense of self? What strategies could you use to cope with this situation? What about when you do not uphold your own values? Can you think of a time when this happened? What caused it to occur? How did you respond? Could you practice taking a few deep breaths to calm yourself if you feel like your value is being challenged?

In Chapter 3 we will explore the importance of boundaries in relationships and maintaining a sense of self, but for now just write down as many coping ideas as you can. For example, is there a phrase you could say to yourself as a reminder of why that value matters to you and why it would be good to stick to it? I call these motivating phrases and I encourage you to write down a motivating phrase for each of your values. Here are some examples.

Value: Family

Motivating phrase: My sense of family gives me a sense of belonging.

Value: Fidelity

Motivating phrase: My fidelity to my partner reflects my commitment to my relationship and helps define my sense of self.

Value: Empathy

Motivating phrase: Through expressing empathy, I demonstrate that I have the courage and resilience to try to stand in someone else's shoes and understand who they are.

Now it's your turn. I myself found this exercise quite hard, but believe me, it is worth it. If we are clear on the importance of our values, we are more likely to demonstrate these values, have a strong sense of self and establish reasonable boundaries.

1. Value: _____

    Motivating phrase: _____

2. Value: _____

    Motivating phrase: _____

3. Value: _____

    Motivating phrase: _____

4. Value: _____

    Motivating phrase: _____

5. Value: _____

    Motivating phrase: _____

6. Value: _____

    Motivating phrase: _____

7. Value: _____

    Motivating phrase: _____

8. Value: _____

   Motivating phrase: _____

9. Value: _____

   Motivating phrase: _____

10. Value: _____

    Motivating phrase: _____

What value did you find in this exercise?

My response: I thoroughly enjoyed this exercise (but I also found it quite hard). I found it helpful to explore my values and discover how they reinforce my sense of self-awareness. I also found it helpful to have a motivating phrase to repeat to myself to help my mind focus upon my values. By focusing on my values, it became easier to routinely demonstrate my values in my day to day life.

Your response:

_____
_____
_____
_____

What did you learn from this exercise?

My response: *I learned that my sense of self-awareness is built upon my ability to know my values and align my beliefs and actions with these values.*

Your response:
_____
_____
_____
_____

Part 2: Beliefs

The next part of this exercise is about your beliefs. When I was young, I repeatedly watched the cartoon *The Little Engine That Could*. In this delightful story, a happy little train carries toys for children to the other side of a mountain. All along this journey, it keeps repeating to itself "I think I can, I think I can, I think I can" while it climbs up the mountain. As it draws to the top of the mountain, the little engine slows down but keeps repeating the words "I think I can, I think I can, I think I can". When at last it finally draws over the top of the mountain, the little engine says as its wheels turn, "I thought I could, I thought I could, I thought I could". As it gathers momentum coming down the mountain, its wheels spin faster and it says, "I thought I could" even faster until, singing its triumph, it rushes on down toward the valley.

I love this story, as it represents that moment in each of us when we stop believing in ourselves, but it also shows us that through practice and resilience, we can change our thoughts and then change our actions. Do take a moment to search for the story on the internet. It is a beautiful story and a childhood favourite of mine. What beliefs do you need to take you over your mountain? And which beliefs are holding you back from climbing your mountain?

Beliefs are thoughts, feelings and assumptions which we hold about ourselves (Jacobson, 2013). These are deeply ingrained and often subconscious. That means we are not fully aware that we hold these beliefs about ourselves. Our beliefs come through in statements or self-talk that we say about ourselves, often subconsciously. This can include such things as:

- I am not good enough
- I am fat
- I am stupid
- No one will ever love me.

These beliefs often stem back to a childhood or past memory and can relate to the way we have chosen to reflect upon that memory. They are like an irrational record stuck on repeat which plays in our minds. Through developing a sense of self-awareness, we can become aware of our negative beliefs, and just like the little engine we can change our beliefs to "I think I can".

What are some of your negative beliefs? Earlier on in the chapter I asked you to reflect upon these. Now I want you to reflect on the following questions. They are adapted from Jacobson (2013).

- Do you think you are confident, clever, pretty, ugly, old, young?
- Are you good at what you do?

- Do you see judgement and criticism in your view of yourself?
- Do you think you are better than everyone else?
- Do you feel worthy of love and happiness?
- Do you think that others are luckier than you?
- Is life easier for other people than it is for you?
- Do you use all or nothing words like *everyone* and *no one*?
- Do you see the world as ugly or beautiful or a mixture of both?
- Do you see other people as good or bad or a mixture of both?

Notice that these questions challenge you to pay attention to whether your beliefs are realistic, positive and reasonable. Self-aware people are aware of their strengths without feeling arrogant. They are also prepared to work on their weaknesses practically and realistically without perceiving themselves as a victim. When we are self-aware, we recognise the greys in life and don't adhere to all or nothing beliefs. What do your answers tell you about some of your negative beliefs?

I want now to help you change these to more positive thoughts and beliefs. I know that in the beginning this may be hard. Remember that you may have held these beliefs for a long time, and just like me you have allowed them to define you. But also just like me and the little engine that could, you can redefine yourself. It just takes practice. Become like the little engine by telling yourself "I think I can" and let's slowly chug up that mountain together. Begin by thinking of five negative beliefs you have about yourself and write them down in the table below. Then, think of a way to reframe these negative, limiting beliefs into more optimistic and realistic beliefs. I've included a couple of examples to get you started.

Negative belief	Reframed positive belief
I am not good enough	I am ok as I am now, but I will continue to develop with each day
I am fat	I am not defined by my body. I am many wonderful things. I choose to decide what I consume and how I care for my body.
No one will ever love me	I am lovable and I am the only one who can define my own worth.
1	
2	
3	
4	
5	

What value did you find in this exercise?

My response: *The value of this exercise for me was that it helped me reframe my thoughts. This means that goals I have set myself have become more achievable and I have a clearer sense of myself. I also identified the importance of holding a balanced rather than all or nothing view of the world.*

Your response:

_____
_____
_____
_____

What did you learn from this exercise?

My response: *I learned that beliefs and thoughts can be limiting and unhelpful, but that once they are reframed, they can open me up to potential positive change and happiness. I realise that practicing this is vital and it is a process which requires skill and determination.*

Your response:

_____
_____
_____
_____

2. Accept yourself

One of my favourite books is the beautiful Australian children's story *The Bunyip of Berkeley Creek* by Jenny Wagner (1973). I loved reading this to my kids. We would read it again and again. For those of you who've never heard the term, a bunyip is a mythical creature from Australian Indigenous mythology. It is notoriously big, ugly and clumsy, and is said to lurk in areas of still water called billabongs. It is my theory that there is a

Chapter 2

bunyip lurking in all of us too. I'll explain why in a moment, but first, let me tell you the tale of *The Bunyip of Berkeley Creek*.

The story begins late one night when the bunyip rises out of the muddy depths of his billabong and commences a search to learn what, or rather who, he is. The bunyip travels through the bush asking all the animals he meets "What am I?" and "Am I handsome?" Several of the animals tell him he is horrible or they say they do not have time for him because they are busy with their own lives. The bunyip is desperately seeking approval and just wants to belong. (Sound familiar?) He continues to travel through the bush, asking various Australian animals about himself, until finally he meets a man. This man is busy and judgmental and does not even look at the bunyip. He decides instead that it 'simply does not exist'. The bunyip eventually leaves this man alone and disappears into the bush. The story tells us that "No one saw him go".

I find these words so significant, as they are true of so much of humanity. Often, we don't take the time to notice and really reflect upon what those around us are experiencing. How do they feel? What are they going through? What can we do for them? This is what it is like for the bunyip who approaches so many animals that have neither time nor empathy for him and do not care for anything beyond the parameters of their own lives. It is such a pity that the animals in the story do not stop to care about the bunyip, but that is how can be in real life too.

The other thing the bunyip does that many of us do too is that he searches for answers to his identity from an outside source, rather than looking within himself. When we ask others who we are, all they can tell us in response is who *they* are. I can see now that this is what it was like for me when I was growing up. I allowed schoolyard bullies and an abusive teacher to negatively affect my sense of self. It was only after a long time that I could reflect on those experiences with insight and observe myself with objectivity. Eventually, I realised that my teacher was damaged and also that she was wrong about me.

Like the bunyip, my need to be accepted throughout much of my life has been driven by wanting to be liked by others. I would continually seek approval and try to behave in ways that would please others rather than be of value to myself. My focus was on being accepted by other people on their terms, rather than simply accepting my SELF and feeling happy with who I was. This applied later in my life too, when I focused my identity on the labels – 'wife', 'mother', 'employee' – that others gave me and which I believed society expected of me. At the time, I thought not only that these labels represented me, but also that upholding them would make me happy. I have since learned, and I hope you will too, that it is only what lies within us that can bring us true happiness, rather than what comes from without.

This is what the bunyip in our story discovers when he at last settles down by a quiet billabong and looks into a mirror. You might say that he uses this mirror to look inside himself. In doing so, he decides that he is a bunyip and he can be as handsome as he likes. He no longer needs approval from society. Instead, he finds his own peace and self-acceptance. Like our lovely bunyip, we all need to take the time to find a quiet place and remind ourselves of who we truly are, without seeking or believing the opinions of those who do not know us.

Exercise 2: On self-acceptance

In the exercise above we looked at reframing our self-talk. Now let's take this a step forward with a role-play to help improve our self-acceptance. The road to self-acceptance begins with intention and making a clear decision. We start by acknowledging our limiting beliefs and then make a concentrated decision to change these beliefs with empathy and care. This exercise is adapted from Fritz Perls' (1977) Gestalt therapy empty chair technique. It is a means of exploring your feelings and beliefs in order to increase your self-awareness and acceptance of yourself today. Now I understand that this will not happen overnight, but the process starts with a decision and with self belief. After that, it requires practice. This exercise deals with expressing empathy in order to process unresolved hurt. Through this, you can increase your self-acceptance.

Here's what you need to do. Get two chairs and place them so they face each other. Then get a teddy bear or some other object to symbolise a caring comforting presence. This roleplay has two steps. First, you are going to sit in one chair and play the role of yourself. The teddy bear or other object in the opposite chair is going to play your caring friend. You are going to talk to the teddy about your past hurts and express how you feel about any judgment or criticism you have experienced. Really explore these feelings with honesty and vulnerability.

Next, you are going to swap chairs so that now you play the role of the caring friend and the teddy plays the role of your vulnerable self. You are going to talk to the teddy as if it is yourself as a child or younger person. You are going to be kind and encouraging toward that younger version of yourself. Using your name, speak gently and lean forward. Demonstrate comforting body language such as nodding your head and saying "I understand. I hear you." Imagine your younger self expressing past hurts and demonstrating vulnerability. This is about allowing yourself to show compassion. Understand the hurt of your younger or vulnerable self, but most of all tell that self to become courageous, assertive and resilient.

Having this conversation back and forth will help you to clarify your feelings, develop perspective and let go. I must admit that when I first tried it, I did feel a little silly. Then I realised that it worked. It helped me to gain perspective and understanding. I could let go of that sad, scared child and could see myself as I really am, which is so much more than a hurt and misunderstood little girl. Quietly, tell your child self that it is ok. Say that the child did the best that he or she could at the time, but now it is time to let go. You may want to hold the teddy's hand or give it a hug. You may choose to use phrases such as the following. (This may be a little confronting so go easy.)

- You will be ok
- I hear you
- That sounds like a difficult experience
- I understand that that would have been hard, but you can do this
- That is most unfortunate, but you have the ability to set boundaries
- I can hear that you felt hurt, but you are not that child any longer
- Take little steps
- I believe in you.

This role-playing exercise can help bring you into the present, and help you heal and reflect with more perspective. It allows you to express understanding and empathy for yourself, which can result in a more rational approach to processing experiences and can lead to self-acceptance.

What value did you find in this exercise?

My response: *For me, the value in this exercise was that it felt healing to take the time to speak to my inner child with kindness and compassion. This gave me the space to view my experiences from another angle and helped me to let go. I realised that I was no longer that abused child and I could be who ever I chose to be. I choose to accept myself.*

Your response:

_____
_____
_____
_____

What did you learn from this exercise?

My response: *I learned that kindness, compassion and letting go are integral to my growth and self-acceptance.*

Your response:

_____
_____
_____
_____

A quick check in

How are you going with the content in this chapter? This is some heavy stuff we are covering, so remember to take it gently. Any time you feel confronted by what you are encountering here, you can always turn to your journal and write out your thoughts. As I have said before, it takes a lot of work to learn to understand and accept yourself. Don't expect it to happen all at once and don't be too hard on yourself. Remember our key concepts. This is a journey and part of the journey is to start noticing things about yourself and about others. This also involves developing different ways of seeing in order to feel happier about yourself and about life in general.

We have already practiced some of these key concepts by reflecting on ourselves and our experiences. We've come to know ourselves better by looking at our values and beliefs, and we have learned a few techniques that may enable us to accept ourselves without needing anyone else's approval. Now we need to look at the final piece of the puzzle, which is to develop ourselves. Let's dive into it.

3. Develop yourself

In the immediate aftermath of my marriage ending, I felt consumed with hurt, blame, and resentment. In time, however, I began to feel that it was important for me to take some responsibility for what happened and to acknowledge what I could have done differently. I understand that there is no use in crying over spilt milk, but there is value in objective reflection. An important part of accepting who we are today is to take a pragmatic and fair minded review of the past. Looking back, I can see that I believed working hard and accumulating wealth and status was of high importance. I now see that experience, health and self-realisation are more meaningful than developing a business, having a beautiful property and driving a nice car. That is not to say that I do not still have things to work on. I am human, after all! I still have weaknesses and I still make mistakes. Today, however, I choose to see these weaknesses and mistakes as opportunities for growth. Through knowing myself and accepting myself, I have the strength to accept changes in my life. I have acquired the insight to develop myself in certain areas with wisdom and kindness.

Exercise 3: Noticing your thoughts

Becoming more aware of your thoughts takes practice. What we are going to do in this exercise is practice slowing down our thoughts long enough to be able to see them differently. With perspective, you can become conscious of what is limiting your self-awareness. By increasing your self-awareness using observation, analysis, changing your internal dialogue and silence, you can start to change your patterns of thought and behaviour. Once we can identify our thoughts, we can make choices about our responses.

At the beginning of this chapter I said that being self-aware means being fully conscious of your fears, your feelings and your thoughts, and then channelling this awareness in a direction which brings you happiness. The purpose of this exercise is for you to learn to map out your thoughts and start to see with perspective the automatic patterns that may repeat in your mind and the effect of these patterns on your self-awareness. Our thoughts create our reality and determine our behaviour. When we realise what triggers our thoughts, we have the power to change them.

I found this exercise really profound and quite surprising as I felt that my thoughts were already aligned with my values.

But when I did this thought map, I realised I needed to further develop my ability to observe my thoughts in order to be able to change my feelings. I found that when I was in the moment by moment hustle and bustle of my life, my mind was like a preset computer program that kept going back into automatic and negative patterns. Some of my negative thoughts were such things as:

- I wonder if she didn't ring me back because she doesn't like me?
- What if no one likes my book?
- Perhaps I am a terrible mother?
- I am too old to change my life.
- My life is just too hard. It will never get easier.

I was quite shocked at some of these thoughts, but the trick in this exercise is to write quickly and not to overthink this. The point is to identify and then change your reactive thoughts. Once I did this, I repeated the exercise and found it increased my ability to observe myself and my journey, rather than just feeling like I was stuck in it.

You need an alarm clock for this one. I use my iPhone with a distinguishing ring tone that sounds like crickets. I want you to set your alarm to go off every hour over a period of five hours across three days. When the alarm sounds, immediately (and I do mean *immediately*) write down what thought you have at that moment. Be precise. Don't change your thought and don't try to adapt it.

Day	Thought one	Thought two	Thought three	Thought four	Thought five
Day 1					
Day 2					
Day 3					

Now I want you to think about these questions:
- What premeditated or triggered these thoughts?
- Were you feeling calm at that time?
- Were you organised?
- Are there any themes here?
- Were you being true to your values?
- What beliefs were driving your thoughts at that time?

For example, I find that my self-esteem and self-awareness are lowest when I have several commitments running at once, which often happens to me as a single mother. I might have school pick up, singing lessons, basketball practice or be driving my children to several different places in a short space of time. Once I recognised that this multitasking could be stressful, I found I could observe my behaviour and be kinder to myself by reorganising things or preparing myself for these busy times. I would also choose to go for a quick walk or meditate after occasions like these and not be so hard on myself. I would consciously observe my thoughts at these more demanding times.

Use the space below to reflect on your own thoughts and what might have caused them.

_____
_____
_____
_____
_____
_____
_____

Now take a moment to think about what you could have done differently at these times. How can you be kind to yourself? Review your responses and commit to making changes where necessary.

_____
_____
_____
_____
_____
_____
_____

What value did you find in this exercise?

My response: *I found this exercise enlightening as I did not realise how automatic my negative thoughts were and was not aware of the particular triggers which motivated these thoughts. Once I observed these patterns, I felt empowered to change them.*

Your response:
_____
_____
_____
_____
_____
_____
_____

What did you learn from this exercise?

My response: *I learned that the practice of observing my thoughts empowered me to change them and I could essentially choose to feel happy.*

Your response:

_____
_____
_____
_____
_____
_____
_____

Your second ritual: Noticing your patterns and reflecting

One of the best ways I have found to develop my self-awareness, self-acceptance and self-understanding is through my practice of rituals. We have yet to explore all the elements that are involved in performing rituals, but you have already made a start by reading or reciting your happiness practice contract from Chapter 1 every day. (You have been doing that, haven't you?) Like that ritual, this one is very simple and you can start doing it right away. All you need to do is to spend a few moments at the end of each day reflecting on what you noticed about yourself that day. When were you aware of your values? Were any of your beliefs strengthened or challenged? Did you feel a sense of self-acceptance or did you let the opinions of others affect how you felt? What steps did you take to develop yourself? What is one thing you could do differently tomorrow to enhance your sense of self-awareness, self-acceptance and self-understanding?

You might like to sit quietly somewhere and ponder these questions. You could write about them in your journal or you could discuss them in conversation with a family member or friend. When you have finished reflecting on your day, you might like to close this ritual by lighting a candle and saying something like, "I am aware of my behaviour today. As the observer, I look upon my behaviour with perspective, and I accept myself as I am right now."

Remember to notice how you feel when you perform your rituals, and write this down in your journal too. Notice in particular any feelings of self doubt or resistance, along with any internal dialogue, and document these. The idea is that through noticing and writing about these things, you will increase your self-awareness and develop skills to manage any negative self-talk.

In a nutshell

Phew! We really went deep in this chapter. Let's recap what we have learned.

- Self understanding and self-acceptance are essential to our happiness, and they both grow from self-awareness.
- Our minds absorb and shape themselves to the stories we tell ourselves.
- Our experiences – like the ones I shared with you through my story – may also shape our sense of self, but we can choose the way we see and process these experiences.
- We don't need to define ourselves according to other people's stories or judgements. Instead, we can create our own.
- The three keys to self-understanding are knowing yourself, accepting yourself and developing yourself.
- Knowing yourself means knowing your values and

beliefs. This includes both limiting beliefs and empowering beliefs.
- Accepting yourself means not relying on others to tell you who you are, but listening instead to that quiet voice inside you.
- Developing yourself means having the insight and kindness to learn from your experiences and to come up with strategies for your 'work on' areas.
- Rituals are a wonderful way to enhance your self-awareness, self-acceptance and self-understanding.

Remember, my friends, when we are self-aware we are better able to understand and accept ourselves. We are also more able to love and to give, and we can place ourselves in a position to let go of what we no longer need. As my father says, if our focus is only upon ourselves, there is no space from which we can give to others. Once we accept ourselves, we can let go of the need to prove that we are worthy. That makes room for us to feel contentment and this means we are more able to give. Speaking of making space, that is what the next chapter is about. In it, we will learn how to create the physical, mindful and social space to allow happiness into our lives.

Chapter 3
CREATE SPACE FOR HAPPINESS

HAVE YOU EVER had a big spring clean of an area of your house and afterwards felt somehow more calm, having more perspective, and feeling more free to be yourself? I know I have. This is one of my favourite topics and also one of my favourite chapters in this book. I say this because it was through consciously creating space in my life that I found happiness could flow in. Not only that, but by doing so, I also realised the tools and strategies I needed in order to maintain that happiness.

Creating space is not just about letting go of stuff. It is also about letting stuff in. It's a bit like clearing out a cluttered room then opening the window right up to let the light stream in so you can marvel at the view. In this chapter, we are going to explore what is involved in creating space for happiness. We will look at how to make the most of the physical, mindful and social spaces in our lives. Of course, we will be referring back to our key concepts and there will be some exercises and a lovely ritual for you to do. I am looking forward to sharing this part of the journey with you because I love creating space for myself – physically, mindfully and socially. I hope you will enjoy it too. There are many wonderful benefits to be found in making space in our lives, so let's begin.

The importance of space

Look around you now. What do you see? Are you in a place that brings you peace? Are there elements of your environment that cause you distress? What are they? You might like to describe what you see out loud to help give you some perspective. How are you feeling? Is your body physically comfortable? Are you hungry or tired? Are any of your muscles clenched? Is your forehead unfurrowed? Are your shoulders relaxed? What about your emotional state? Do you feel content, curious, alert? Are you alone or are there other people around? Do you feel close to these people? Is there ease or tension between you? What do you notice about the space within you and around? What feels good about it? Have a think about these questions. Perhaps you could brainstorm some thoughts in your journal. We will be doing an exercise soon which relates back to these questions.

This idea of space is really important to me because for much of my life, I simply did not allow myself any room for happiness. I was too busy rushing around, keeping fit for my next triathlon, trying to find or keep a relationship, seeking approval from others, gaining another qualification, holding onto the past, and worrying obsessively about the future. Does this sound like you? So many of us have lives like this. We are busy, distracted and bouncing around without any true focus or clarity. We keep looking towards a brighter future that never seems to arrive, rather than experiencing happiness in the now. We allow ourselves to be drawn into other people's stories. We ruminate, we obsess and we overthink our lives. On top of that, we fill our physical environment with all kinds of possessions. We fill our bodies with junk. We try to cram so much into every single day that our lives end up being overcrowded. It is no wonder we lack the space to be happy.

Space can be defined as being a continuous area or expanse which is free and available. Just think about those words 'free' and 'available' for a moment. What do they mean to you? How do you feel when you say them out loud? What images appear in your mind? For me, I imagine feeling free to love, free to run, free to be myself, and free to be available to possibility and opportunity. I visualise myself walking along the beach, holding hands with a friend, playing with my children, or laughing with friends. I also imagine a spacious room with natural light streaming in as I meditate in contentment. You might like to write about your responses to these words or draw images of them in your journal. Ask yourself if you have a sense of freedom and availability in your life.

Often we end up being distracted and cluttered by habits, objects, people and places that take us away from ourselves and our happiness. So how do we get this back? How do we get back to our true selves? When we create space, it is like pruning back an overgrown tree and seeing the sun shine through the branches. When we clear away the physical and emotional clutter in our lives, we are making room to focus upon one sensation at a time. We allow ourselves the calmness and clarity to practice the art of noticing and to become fully aware of ourselves and our surroundings. We also rediscover what really matters to us and can begin to see who we really are.

As I went through the process of grieving after my marriage ended, there were several stages when I needed to create space in order to heal and be happy. I kept so much stuff from my marriage. I had in a treasured box every card and letter my ex-husband ever sent me, along with gifts and other things which reminded me of my married life. And yes, at times

Chapter 3

I would look inside this box and reminisce. Sometimes it is positive to hold on to memories, but in this situation, all this stuff was taking up space and keeping me stuck in the past. It was cluttering up my mind and stopping me from moving on. On one occasion, one of my friends pointed in frustration at a wedding picture still displayed on the kitchen buffet and said, "For heaven's sake, get that dinosaur out!" After a while, my girlfriends began coming over to my house to help me declutter. With their assistance, I cleared out the house and let go of the things I no longer needed. The funny thing was that as much as I felt better when I decluttered and gave things away, it was still hard for me to let go. I think this is because we sometimes allow our emotional baggage to define us so much that we almost become attached to it. I think that's what it was like for me.

The decluttering process took weeks and required a lot of sorting, sifting and throwing away. With each decision I made to donate or discard items, it felt like I was creating more space. This was not only physical space, but emotional and mindful space too. It felt that by clearing my physical environment, I was opening my mind to experience comfort and happiness again. As I said, the decision to give things away was not always easy. Actually, at times I felt sad and wanted to hold on, but with practice it became easier. It was like saying goodbye to a part of myself, but it allowed me to review my life with more perspective. I realised that the more I held on, the less likely it was that my life would move on. As with most change, there was a grieving or letting go period, and that is ok. I rearranged the furniture to allow light, opportunity and positive thoughts to flow into my home. Before long, my house seemed friendlier and more inviting. It felt like a space which reflected who I was now, rather than who I had been in my past. It felt good to be in it.

I created special spaces for my children so they each had a place where they could go to meditate, reflect and just be. I named each space and made sure they were warm and welcoming and reflected on who my children are. Each space had meaning. Through making these changes, we started to move on as a family. As I touched the various things in my life and moved them or threw them away, I felt lighter. As I created a dedicated space for meditation and yoga, I felt full of purpose. As I organised photos, I felt a sense of release. As I stilled the internal dialogue of my mind, I felt open to opportunity. I stopped ruminating on the past and began to concentrate on what really matters. And I began feeling happier.

You may not have the same experience as I did, but I know that a big part of my happiness today comes from the space I have created. This process was so cleansing for me, and I'm excited for you to get started on it too. We will start with your physical environment, but there is more to it than that. For you to feel happy and practice your rituals, you need to attend to your emotional and social spaces too. This involves reflecting on the activity of your mind and becoming aware of how people, relationships and places affect your wellbeing.

Physical space

Do you like watching reality TV shows? Friends of mine love to watch the ones about watching people learn how to cook and serve meals to guests. Well, thanks to a man called Graham Hill, I now like to watch life editing shows. I enjoy shows, blogs, and videos on how to declutter and adapt your use of space in order to allow happiness in. Graham is one of my TED Talk mentors with his mantra of 'less stuff, more happiness' (Hill, 2011). He started a project called Life Edited (see lifeedited.com), which is all about designing your life so you have

Chapter 3

more happiness, health and money by using less stuff, space and energy. After watching Graham Hill's TED Talk, I immediately subscribed to the Life Edited newsletter. Something about watching people give stuff away and declutter their lives makes me feel like I am also decluttering my life.

Graham describes simplifying our physical space as being like 'clearing the arteries of our lives' (Hill, 2011). He says we need to shift away from the belief which currently dominates Western societies that collecting is cool and accumulating more is better. Instead, he suggests we need to change our way of seeing and start viewing 'less' as the new 'sexy'. There is a moment in his TED Talk when Graham encourages us to ask ourselves if each item that we store is really going to make us happier. I am fascinated by this question. I have watched Graham's talk several times and have encouraged my children to watch it too. I can't help thinking that if a possession is not making us happy, then it may very well be a distraction from our happiness.

Inspired by Graham, I ruthlessly edited my life. Out went so many of my clothes, my shoes, my papers, my containers, along with a lot of stuff in the pantry and the garage. Now, I don't want you to think that after all these efforts I have it all under control. (I have four kids, remember!) But, as I mentioned above, this process of decluttering has given me an enormous sense of freedom. The more stuff I gave away, the freer I felt. And then I started noticing things. With the space I cleared in my bathroom after getting rid of the perfumes, the shampoos and the electric toothbrush, I saw the need for a couple of plants. These plants have now become the feature in a simply decorated room. Not only have they given me so much more happiness than the array of perfumes and trinkets I used to display, but the bathroom itself has become a calm sanctuary. As a result, my morning rituals have become a more spiritual experience.

I also gave away a lot of clothes and suddenly realised how beautiful the ones I kept are. I gave away several of the remaining things that my ex-husband had given me, and by letting them go I not only released pent up feelings, but was reminded how special he had been to me. All of these things brought me more freedom. In particular, it gave me the freedom to be me. I saw how little I really needed to be happy. With less stuff, I am more able to keep my life streamlined and allow my environment to match my values.

Graham Hill postulates that intentionally creating our spaces in this way will give us more freedom and more time. Being an architect, he is thinking of physical space but he also talks about the effect that creating space can have on the mind. (More on that later.) Graham suggests three ways in which we can create space and free up our minds:

1. **Edit ruthlessly** by cutting back what is not essential and stopping the inflow of the unnecessary
2. **Think small** and be efficient by only buying items for a specific purpose and not simply to acquire them
3. **Make things multifunctional**, such as having a coffee table that also serves as a dinner table.

Be honest. How many of these things are you doing right now? Can you think of ways to start applying these principles in your life? What changes could you make in your behaviour or your space to reflect these values? Think about these questions in your journal. Of course, there is more to the idea of physical space than just our external surroundings. To really experience spaciousness, we need to look inside too.

During the writing of this book, I found myself really noticing how I felt physically in certain environments. I observed that my body had a natural, in-built radar for uncertainty and stress. Sometimes when I lacked the ability to assess the negativity of a certain environment, I would simply pay attention to my body to see how it felt about the situation. I noticed when I felt negative that my forehead might become furrowed, my throat would sometimes constrict, my hips would get tight, or my shoulders would hunch up. By taking care of our bodies, we can finely tune our physical awareness and use it to assess – and also enjoy – the spaces we occupy.

Your physical space within

I recently competed in a natural bodybuilding competition. It was the ninth time I have entered such a competition. I find the preparation I do gives me time to reflect and the training enables my body to feel mobile and supple. I enjoy the routine and structure. It helps me to remember my body is the temple to my mind and having a healthy, fit body helps to keep my mind clear. I develop rituals for my nutrition and exercise. These keep me focused and give me the structure I need when working towards such a big goal. From Sunday to the end of Friday I eat clean, which means I don't eat anything that contains colourings, sauces, preservatives or refined sugars. I call Saturday my 'cheat' day. On this day, I allow myself to eat anything.

You may not aspire to compete in bodybuilding competitions, but even so, you do need to give your body some attention to keep it healthy and strong. Here are some ways you can do this:

1. Engage in achievable exercise, like walking, gardening or weightlifting.

2. Drink water regularly.
3. Eat a healthy diet and cut back on refined sugars, processed and packaged foods.
4. Meditate.
5. Practice yoga or a mobility routine such as stretching or pilates.
6. Practice the art of noticing.
7. Avoid recreational drugs, including tobacco.
8. Drink alcohol in moderation.
9. Structure your use of the internet. The internet provides information and news at a rate too fast for us to absorb quietly and without balance. This means that we may end up viewing a disproportionate amount of negative information. Diarise your internet and social media time and stick to it.
10. Spend time with life- and like-minded positive people. (Yes, I did say 'life-minded'. This means people who appreciate being alive.)
11. Pay attention to your breath.

Some of you might be surprised to read that last suggestion, but the patterns of our breathing tell so much about who we are. My breathing rituals are among the most important ones in my practice. When our lives get overcrowded and we are distracted, it is almost as if we become closed in and end up fighting to breathe. If I feel myself getting overwhelmed, one of the first things I notice is that my breathing becomes restricted and my throat tightens up. This is why I thought we would start the exercises in this chapter with one of my favourite breathing practices to open up our airways and centre ourselves.

CHAPTER 3

Exercise 1: Life-source breathing exercise

This is a pranayamic inspired breathing exercise to help you create the space to be in the moment. I find pranayamic breathing to be incredibly healing in my own journey, especially when I feel overwhelmed or I lack balance. *Prana* is a Sanskrit (ancient language of India) word for 'life force', and *yama* means 'to control'. Pranayama therefore means regulating the breath or respiration. The way we do this is through the formal practice of exercises that control the breath in order that we may feel aware, in the present moment, and vital. Prana or life force enters the body through the action of breathing. Likewise, breath is life – not just physically, but emotionally and spiritually as well. According to ancient Indian belief, if the prana level is high and its flow is continuous and unencumbered, the mind remains calm, positive and motivated. However, due to lack of practice and attention to one's breath, the breath may become restricted or limited. When our breathing does become restricted, feelings of anxiety and fear or a lack of self-awareness may increase. By practicing pranayamic breathing, you are essentially increasing your lung capacity and learning to sit with the experience of each breath.

Please be aware that the practice of pranayama is an ancient practice and requires skill. The reason I would like to use a pranayamic inspired exercise here is the pattern of our breath and the amount of lung capacity we use tells us so much about our awareness of our surroundings, our space and our self. Inspired by pranayamic breathing techniques, I call this exercise life-source breathing because it reminds us that we are alive now and brings us back to the source – which is ourselves. Breathing is one physical act which clearly relates a physical action to our emotional state. Long-term practice can help with our focus and self-awareness. This exercise is intended to be both physical and mindful. It is suitable for beginners, although I must admit that it is also one I do daily.

Before you start

As with any physical practice, it is a good idea to consult your doctor before you start this pranayamic inspired breathing. There are also some environmental requirements you will need to put in place before you begin. It is better to be in a comfortable environment with a room temperature that is neither too hot nor too cold. Make sure your airways are open and spacious. Blow your nose before you start so the air passages are clear for nasal breathing. And of course, don't practice if you are feeling unwell. Pay attention to how you sit, whether that is on a chair or cross legged on the floor or a cushion, and keep your back straight. Remember that your practice is just that: a practice. Start with one to two minutes a day. Yes, you read correctly. I did say one to two minutes a day. This is not about quantity; it is about practice and quality. There are so many times throughout my day that I sit down for one minute and consciously do life-source breathing.

Instructions

As you sit quietly and breathe, imagine an open space and visualise the journey of the breath and the life force energy that is created through the act of nasal breathing. Really notice the here and now and connect this sense of presence to each breath. As you find your breath slowing down, gradually notice your chest, your throat, your limbs and other areas of your body separately and with focus, then let each one go. Allow yourself to physically let go of the whole of your body as one. Feel the life force of breath touch and revitalise each part of the body. Give particular focus to your heart space, which is the area around your heart. This is the source of self-awareness and compassion. Sometimes I may place my left hand for a moment upon my own heart space to feel my heartbeat as I focus on the rise and fall of my chest with each breath. I find this works as a trigger for me to let go. Become aware of the relaxed sensation in your body and consciously allow that feeling to travel down your spine. During this time imagine space, infinite space, stillness and quiet. Inner calmness will then be experienced.

I want you to pause now and just observe your breath. Notice its quality and length, without any judgment or expectation. What is it telling you? Notice the effect of lengthening and deepening the breath. How does this pattern of breathing make you feel? Practice the art of noticing your breathing around particular places, spaces and people. Record your observations in your journal. Try to tune in to what your breath is telling you. When we are happy, our breath is unimpeded. Our self-awareness is at one with our physical self. By breathing and taking the time to be still, we can create the mindful space within us to allow us to feel happy.

What value did you find in this exercise?

My response: *There are just so many benefits in this exercise from the simple focus upon stillness, which reduces stress and increases a sense of contentment, to the benefit of teaching us to observe our physical and emotional self with detachment, giving us a renewed sense of perspective.*

Your response:

_____
_____
_____
_____
_____
_____
_____

What did you learn from this exercise?

My response: *I love this exercise as it always lifts my mood. I learned that a simple exercise such as focusing on my breath can bring me back into touch with the present and help me to notice the simple joys of life which are all around me.*

Your response:

_____
_____
_____
_____
_____
_____
_____

CHAPTER 3

Your physical space without

What did you think of that life-source breathing practice? I do hope you found it calming. Now that you are feeling more relaxed and centred, let's revisit some strategies to help you declutter your physical surroundings. Much of this chapter has already discussed the wonderful rewards of cleaning up and clearing out your space. In addition to the ideas that have already been proposed, here are some other suggestions to encourage you to create and maintain your physical surroundings:

1. Assess your possessions and get rid of anything that isn't used or doesn't make you happy.
2. Only buy what you actually need.
3. Pay attention to what you collect. Does that collection really give you joy? Perhaps hold various items in your hand and ask yourself if it is helping bring you happiness today.
4. Get into the garden or spend time in some other outdoor space. Notice the cycle of life. Feel the earth upon your hands and touch the trees and plants.
5. Create an altar of objects, symbols and items which have meaning for you or which simply make you feel good.
6. Encourage natural light into your living space. (I love this one.)
7. Resist the urge to fall prey to brand marketing. Does that miracle cream really work and contain ingredients you can believe in?
8. Recycle. Try not to add to landfill, but be creative and reuse where possible.

9. Be mindful of the environment and watch your carbon footprint.
10. Dedicate particular spaces to particular practices, whether this is eating or sleeping or exercising.

Again, this last point is one I would like to explore further, as it is a really important part of creating a happy physical space. It is not enough that the space is neat and uncluttered. It also has to have purpose and meaning. One way to achieve this is by making sure that certain spaces are consciously used for certain activities. Soon I will invite you to create a space that is specially designated for your happiness. First, though, I want to talk about the importance of symbols.

Happy symbols

Did you have a favourite soft toy or teddy as a child? My son loves his big teddy. He sleeps with it every night, cuddles it, dresses it and speaks to it. Even as adults, we still have our teddies. These are things which give us comfort and have sentimental meaning to us. Perhaps our particular teddy is an old cardigan, a treasured blanket, a chair by the fire, or our special tea cup. These objects are meaningful because they convey comfort, which you will remember is one of the three ways we experience happiness. In some ways, they act as symbols for this happiness.

Like rituals, symbols are very important in our lives. We may have cultural or religious symbols in our lives as well as personal ones that enable us to feel comfort, connection and reward. What is important about symbols is that they are suited to you and reflect who you are. They may include things like photos, plants or mementoes. They might relate to particular colours or the wearing of certain clothing. We can use these symbols to help us focus on our sense of self and on being in the moment. They can also stand as an outward sign of an inner experience. In this case, that inner experience is happiness. When we consciously surround ourselves with such symbols, we are reminding ourselves of our commitment to be happy. What symbols bring you this feeling of happiness? Perhaps you would like to note these down in your journal?

Some of my symbols include:

- Candles
- Incense
- A comfy windcheater
- Ornaments such as a Buddha statue or a statue of Jesus
- Oil burner and oils
- My tropical rainforest of bathroom plants
- Salt lamps
- Fluffy slippers
- My favourite tea cup
- The tree of life symbol (ring, necklace, picture)
- Family photos
- My beautiful, ornate handcrafted mirror from Malaysia, which has a story behind it and which I occasionally stand in front of. I speak to my reflection and remind myself of my worth

Having these symbols around me brings to my mind their meaning. Each time I see or touch them, I am reminded of my commitment to myself to be happy.

Exercise 2: Create your happy space

Remember that quiet billabong the bunyip in Chapter 2 found? It was the place where he could simply be himself, without needing to worry about what society thought of him. We all need a place like that and in this exercise, you are going to create your own happy space. To give you some ideas for your happy space, let me tell you about mine. It is my chair next to the window. I sit in it with the blinds open and look out at the trees. From my window, I can see a glimpse of the sea and the buildings of Melbourne. Sometimes I burn a candle while I sit here or I have a plant nearby. There is no clutter in this space and I bring to it only things that give me those precious feelings of comfort, engagement and reward. I love to sit here, sipping tea from my favourite cup.

Your happy space is an area in which you can play and be yourself. This could be somewhere inside your house, a spot in your garden or a place on your balcony. The important ingredient here is that you dedicate this area as your happy place and aim to keep it private, tranquil and clutter-free. Where possible, go for soft or natural lighting, with no fluorescents. Avoid having electronic gadgets and technological or communication devices in your space, except perhaps something that will let you play music. Try to include something that helps you connect with nature. This could be a plant or an object made from stone or wood. Maybe you would like to have fresh flowers here or bring in other beautiful aromas.

Before you start to create your happy place, have a think about the questions I asked earlier. How do you feel right now in your space? Make some notes in your journal. Especially notice how your current space makes you feel. The happy space you create does not need to be large, but it does need to feel special. Choose some happy symbols to bring into this space. Select and arrange these items to ensure that the environment is not distracting and helps to clarify rather than crowd your mind. This is your space, away from the madding crowds and away from everyone else's opinions. It is a place for self-expression and self-inquiry, where you can go to create, reflect, meditate, throw out a yoga mat, write in your journal, plan, and even dream.

Once you have created your space, set some boundaries around it. These might relate to the times or the ways in which you use the space. For instance, when you enter your happy space, you might like to take a soft brush and symbolically sweep away your worries and concerns. You can use your hand for this gesture but, as we have discussed above, it is nice to have a symbol. Another thing you might like to do is to cover your shoulders with a cloth or blanket when you are in your happy space. This can symbolise comfort, like a baby being wrapped in swaddling, and may give you the sensation of feeling cosy, warm and secure. Remember that your happy space is your own. Take the time to make it special. Focus on your feelings and let it be like a gift you are giving yourself.

What value did you find in this exercise?

My response: *The value of this exercise was that it made me realise the importance of creating a simple space of my own in which I may reflect, meditate or heal. I also found it beneficial to use hand-picked symbols for comfort as this gave me a sense of power over my feelings and environment. I realised that I could choose my feelings.*

Your response:

_____
_____
_____
_____
_____
_____
_____

What did you learn from this exercise?

My response: *I have learned that creating a dedicated happy space can increase my happiness and comfort through giving me a sense of meaningful simplicity. The knowledge that I myself have created this special space and that it inherently reflects who I am reinforces this sense of tranquil comfort. In making this place mine through the use of meaningful symbols, I have learned that a simple space can be empowering by imparting a sense of security, safety and meaning. It feels a little like when I used to hide from the world in a homemade tent as a child. Even though the sheets tied in knots were hardly a barricade from the outside world, they still gave me the sense of a safe and healing space.*

Your response:

_____
_____
_____
_____
_____
_____

The link between physical and mental spaces

The benefit of consciously creating our physical space is that it can act as a mirror of how we feel and also be a stimulus for our internal state. If our physical space enables us to reflect and be silent, then we will more easily find the mental space to reflect and be silent. Likewise, if we clutter our space, we will clutter our minds and stem the flow of our being. When we clear our minds, we can find the space to truly feel, experience and appreciate our lives. This is about creating mindful space by choosing what we fill our minds with. Let's look now at how we can make that happen.

Mindful space

When I refer to mindful space, I am speaking of the mental or conscious space of our minds. It is our self-awareness which affords us acceptance, knowledge, perception and the ability to develop and be resilient. Our minds are manifested through our thoughts, feelings and language. Creating space in the mind allows us the room to understand and process in order to create meaning. Awareness is the key here. This comes with quiet and a focus that is simple and uncluttered. Such focus is trained and concentrated, but carries with it no stress or anxiety. Instead, it is about being fully conscious in the moment and in what is happening right now, so that we may feel and experience the present.

We have all heard the idea that our minds are so powerful our beliefs can affect us both mentally and physically. One extreme example of this is found in the ritual in Indigenous Australian culture known as 'pointing the bone'. In this ritual, a specially prepared bone is pointed at a chosen victim. The requirement is that the victim needs to believe in the power of the ritual. Within a period of days, the victim becomes ill and wastes away. In some cases, the victim even dies, apparently from psychosomatic causes. In other words, the person believes strongly enough that they are going to become sick and maybe die, and within days of having the bone pointed at them, they do so.

Our minds are infinitely powerful in this way and our feelings are a direct reflection of our beliefs, our thoughts and our internal dialogue. If we believe that something will hurt us, it will. Equally, if we believe that something will make us happy, it will. As you learned in the previous chapter, I believed for most of my life that I was, as my teacher taught me, mentally slow. I allowed this belief to dictate many of my decisions and expectations. I assumed people would think me stupid and I told myself that I could not write. It was not until I changed my way of thinking that I found the space to believe – and to behave – differently. The fact that you are reading this book shows you how valuable it can be for us to allow room for new ideas and new attitudes in our minds.

Happiness researcher Shawn Achor describes about our mind's desire to seek, create and repeat patterns (One Day University, 2010). This tendency in us is so strong, according to Achor, that after a while, our mind will look for and follow a pattern, even if that pattern is not in our best interest. Psychologist William James (as cited in Cordeschi, 2002, p. 36) in his classic book *Habit* describes this tendency as being like water that "in flowing, hollows out for itself a channel, which grows broader and deeper; and after having ceased to flow, it resumes, when it flows again, the path traced by itself before". In other words, our minds are designed to recreate and remember these learned patterns naturally and instinctively. This can be a good thing but it can also be a bad one. It is important to recognise this inclination of our mind and use it to our advantage.

Obsession, addiction and distraction

In our search for feelings of comfort, engagement and reward, we may find that we become obsessed, addicted or have an unhealthy attachment to certain pursuits. I understand that these pursuits may give us the feeling that they are filling a hole in our lives but really they are taking up the space we need in order to let happiness in. Rather than giving us a sustainable experience of being happy, these obsessions and addictions distract us away from self-inquiry and our awareness of the present moment. Some examples of these pursuits include:

1. Shopping
2. Television
3. Video games
4. Food
5. Drugs
6. Alcohol

7. Sex
8. Internet
9. Social media.

Each of us will have a different relationship to these and similar activities, so you need to ask yourself when these pursuits are useful and when they become destructive. Of course, recreational drugs are always destructive. Yet equally, there are times when shopping may be an engaging and joyful activity. The question to ask is where the line is for you. This is where the concept of reflection can be so useful. It can help you recognise positive and negative behaviours. Being honest about your addictions is really important here. I am not saying you should never shop, drink or even collect things. My dear cousin Lona, for instance, has the most amazing collections of photos displayed around her home and stored in albums. These photos hold special meaning in her life. She is an avid photographer and says that her downtime or 'me' time is often spent with a cup of tea sorting through her photos. My cousin says she enjoys the sensations of touching the photos and turning the pages over as she reflects on happy memories and stages of her children's lives. This ritual adds to the quality of my cousin's life.

The point here is awareness and not allowing your behaviours to control you or distract you from being with yourself. When we give away control over our state of being, either to other people or to distractions like these, we also give away our power to decide to live a contented life. Happiness ALWAYS comes from within and not from obsessively needing something beyond ourselves. Remember that, my friends, and choose wisely. And if you are facing a serious addiction that is affecting your wellbeing, please seek professional help.

Ways to create mindful space

The good news is that there are many positive behaviours and activities you can engage in to help you find that precious mindful space which will contribute to your happiness. Here is a list of some of my favourites. Perhaps there is something here that you might like to try too.

1. Meditation (of course!)
2. Journaling (yes, it is one of my all time faves)
3. Undertaking actions and behaviours which benefit others
4. Developing social relationships which support intimacy, engagement and bonding
5. Finding inspiration through reading books on philosophy and self-development
6. Taking enjoyment in natural beauty and contributing to environmental sustainability
7. Having a plan towards self-improvement (because you know I love a plan!)
8. Taking time for peaceful reflection
9. Supporting actions which encourage resilience and discourage racism, discrimination and marginalisation by promoting a sense of community, such as supporting neighbourhood groups or participating in activities which promotes communal behaviours
10. Resolving conflicts before the sun goes down (as my mum taught me to do)
11. Cultivating kindness and compassion through daily rituals (see Chapter 4 for more details on this)

12. Visualising joyful memories, inspiring dreams and motivating goals.

Did any of those resonate with you? Are there some you are already doing or any that sound tempting? Get out your journal and write down your own list of meaningful and enjoyable ways for you to create mindful space. As you write, you might notice that some of the items on your list relate to the values you identified in Chapter 2. This is another thing you could write about in your journal. Make a commitment to yourself to reduce the behaviours and activities that clutter your mind, and focus instead on those that make you feel more free and available.

Seeing mindfully

I am sure it is becoming clear to you that the creation of mindful space involves many of the concepts and practices we have already discussed. These include journaling and meditating, along with the art of noticing. Our way of seeing becomes relevant here too, as we learn to shift our attention away from worry and negativity towards peace and resilience instead. Some of this relates to the ideas about self-acceptance that we covered in Chapter 2, but there is more to it than that. How often do we lose touch with the happiness available to us in any given moment because we are consumed with anxiety about the future or burdened by concerns from the past? I know this has been true for me.

Some of the happiest moments of my life have at times been squashed under the enormous weight of wondering 'what if?' and worrying about money or time or other issues. I remember when my eldest daughter was born, I looked at her through the plastic crib in the hospital and thought that I loved her so much. I was overwhelmed with love. But instead of simply marvelling in the beauty and wonder of each one of her tiny breaths, I kept thinking, "What if I am not good enough? What if I can't give her enough? What if I can't earn enough money to support us?" Instead of getting wrapped up in this kind of unhelpful speculation, we need to stop, take a breath, and return our focus to the here and now.

Brother David Steindl-Rast (2013), monk and interfaith scholar, speaks about how he just sits in the moment and pays attention to such simple things as having running water or turning on a switch to light up a room. He feels such gratitude for these experiences and really takes the time to notice them. You can be like Brother David too. You can choose to observe more, notice more and appreciate more in every moment. When I was married and we lived on our magnificent property, it was often freezing. We didn't have any heating and were sometimes without water. These days when I wake, I place my feet upon warm and thick wool carpets. I feel their texture under my toes, and immediately I feel grateful. What is the first thing you notice when you wake up each day? What do you feel grateful for?

We have the ability to empower our thoughts and actions through what we notice and how we choose to see. For instance, if we decide to view life through an optimistic lens, we are far more likely to behave in ways that encourage good fortune. That doesn't mean we delude ourselves, however. The key to seeing life with optimism is to be realistic about it at the same time.

Realistic optimism

A big part of finding happiness is accepting that life is not always fair and the world does not owe us a living. I was speaking with a dear friend recently when she asked, "Don't you feel that we all deserve happiness?" This prompted me to think about the concept of 'deserving' something or feeling that we have an entitlement or right to a relationship, situation or item. Maybe years ago I believed that I 'deserved' happiness, but now I feel that life just doesn't work that way. The simple truth is that life can be hard. It is often unfair and at times quite cruel, but we need to find ways to feel happy anyway. There is never going to be a perfect moment to feel happy. As we learned in Chapter 1, it is about beginning where you are. So why not replace any thoughts of "I deserve happiness" with ones that say "I decide to be happy, no matter what". That can be harder than it sounds, but it doesn't mean we should give up. Quite the opposite, in fact. As I have said before in this book (and will keep on saying), if our happiness depends upon fairness, justice or other people's behaviours, then we will never be truly happy. Yet when we see that the answers lie within our own minds, we are more able to find opportunity in the face of cold, hard reality. That is where realistic optimism comes in.

Being a realistic optimist is about seeing our ability to change and then taking practical action to make that change. I have a colleague who admittedly has had a difficult life, but constantly says things like "This is ridiculous", "That's not fair" or "This is just not right". Such views waste so much time and energy (in my opinion) with the result of feeling frustrated, bitter or resentful. Rather than focusing on fairness or luck, which are beyond our control, it is about saying things like "I will restructure myself and work differently in order to achieve my goals" or "I will use this hiccup to regroup and improve".

Focus on what you can change and accept, or choose to withdraw from what you cannot control. It is about having self belief, but also about reflecting, planning and preparing in support of this, and then developing the tools and doing the work to make things happen. We all aspire to be happy, but many of us spend our time just dreaming and wishing, rather than deciding and doing. Being a realistic optimist means having clear, no-nonsense goals, values and systems while remaining hopeful and in the present. I believe that a realistic grasp on how to feel happy comes from assessing ground zero and dealing with it, practically, positively and methodically. Therefore, our happiness is not just about the goal or the destination, but also about the tools and strategies we use to get there.

We can still have our dreams and aspirations, but we need to get real and back those dreams with belief, processes and planning, and we need to cultivate an attitude of optimism. Fortunately, the esteemed Martin Seligman (2010) says that we can learn to be optimistic. It is simply a matter of "learning a new set of cognitive skills" (Seligman, 2010, p. 19). You have already begun practicing a number of these skills, such as noticing, reflecting and reframing your thoughts and your self-talk to be more positive. There is another mind tool that can also contribute to your optimism and your outlook. It is one I use a lot and I'm excited to share it with you.

Visualisation

Let me tell you, my friends, I am a big one for mental imagery. I believe we are so much more likely to reach our destination when we can clearly map out the route and see the landmarks of our journey. The key to achieving a state of happiness could lie in your ability to visualise it or create a mental picture of it that is complete in every detail. By visualising ourselves as being happy, we are more likely to really experience that happiness when it occurs. We can also use visualisation to get ready to face any challenges that may arise for us. If we think ahead, we can prepare ahead and develop strategies to overcome adversity.

I should explain that visualisation is a little different to meditation, as it is about a virtual experience. Even though the word 'visualisation' implies it is visual, the practice is most effective when it employs all of your senses. This means that as well as 'seeing' your visualisation, you can also smell, taste, hear and even touch it. You use your imagination to create and experience these details. For example, you might visualise yourself being at the sea. You can see the glint of sunlight on the water. You can smell and taste the salt in the air. You can hear the waves washing up on the shore and you can feel the sand between your toes. Or you might imagine yourself sitting down to dinner with people you love. Can you picture the table setting? Can you hear the conversation and laughter, and smell and taste the food? Can you feel yourself smiling as you look into the face of each guest and listen to them speak? How does the room feel? Is it warm or cool? How does your body feel with these people in this space?

Using guided imagery like this is a excellent technique for happiness and stress management. When you visualise happiness, you are teaching your body and mind to feel happier outside of the visualisation. By repeatedly imagining yourself performing certain acts or experiencing particular feelings, you may be able to condition your neural pathways to do and feel these more easily in your everyday life. This next exercise shows you how to do this.

CHAPTER 3

Exercise 3: Visualising happiness

In this exercise, I want you to think about a time when you felt happy. It could be a recent event or something from a long time ago. Begin by making sure you are comfortable and relaxed, with a straight back so you are giving your lungs room to breathe. Take a moment to focus on your breath. Inhale and exhale deeply. Close your eyes and just let your mind and body settle. Now I want you to visualise that happy time in your life. Picture it in as much detail as you can. Remember the colours you could see and the time of day. Think about who you were with and what was around you. Then start to bring in your other senses. Can you hear any sounds? Are they near or far? Loud or soft? What can you smell? Is there a taste associated with that memory? Can you bring that taste into your mind now? What about textures? What can you feel under your feet? What can you touch with your hands? What feeling do you have against your skin?

Let yourself sink into this experience. Recreate all the little details. Let your mind roam freely through your memory of that occasion. Let your senses delight in it once more. Visualise now your actions at that time. Perhaps you were walking or talking with friends. Imagine each action separately and focus on the image and feeling of the individual movements. Imagine this in slow motion to heighten your senses even more. Hear everything. Smell everything. Taste everything. Feel everything. Focus now on the feeling of happiness in your body. You might experience this as lightness or warmth. You might feel a sense of peace or joy. Focus on that feeling. Is it located somewhere in particular?

Now I want you to open yourself up to possibility. Imagine that feeling of happiness is spreading throughout your body. Let yourself really feel this happiness. The feeling is so strong that it crowds out all other feelings and it puts all else into perspective. No longer does local gossip or someone else's petty judgment have meaning for you. It is simply drowned out. This feeling of happiness is comforting. You feel a sense of self-acceptance and a sense of belonging to something greater than yourself. How does it affect your physical self? What about your emotional self? Notice your body when you feel happy. I want you to really explore, feel and become aware these feelings. Notice, observe, witness. Feel that happiness within you and know that it is available to you at any time. Then, when you are ready, come back into the present moment, bringing with you these feelings of gratitude, compassion, peace and humility.

What value did you find in this exercise?

My response: *The value of this exercise is that it teaches me how to create, control, and design my own feelings of happiness through the infinite power of my mind. I learned that I hold the power to ultimately decide how to feel.*

Your response:

_____
_____
_____
_____
_____
_____

What did you learn from this exercise?

My response: I learned that I have some control over my happiness. I have learned that happiness is a feeling and I control how much I feel and notice each experience of it. I realised that my imagination is an incredibly powerful tool and that I can learn to enhance certain feelings by focusing on them while minimising others – like turning the volume up or down on a TV.

Your response:

_____
_____
_____
_____
_____
_____

A quick check in

Did you enjoy that visualisation? Could you feel that happiness in your body? This is one of the wonderful ways we can create mindful space. You can use this technique to picture yourself in a future situation, such as when you have an important event to attend or will be spending time with people. So far in this chapter, we have learned that happy people create physical environments that support and enhance their happiness. They develop their minds to focus on the positives and become aware of the present moment. Another thing happy people do is that they dedicate themselves to meaningful social interaction while maintaining healthy boundaries. That is what we are going to consider next.

Social space

This idea of social space is precious to me because I have had a repeated pattern of trying too hard to please the partners in my life at the expense of my sense of self. Has that ever happened to you? In the past, I have not always recognised when it is time to gently walk away, and have undervalued myself in the process. Notice that I use the word 'gently' here, as this is a key concept for me when considering boundaries. Through experience (and making mistakes along the way), I have learned that the most reasonable life choices are made without reacting, but with calm contemplation and perspective. No, don't be silly, of course I am not calm all the time! But I have come to believe that a gentle, carefully considered decision is generally better than a passionate or reactive one.

This part of the book is about creating space in order that we can feel free to define ourselves, set healthy boundaries, and enjoy our relationships. In many ways, this section on social space could be a book in itself, but for now I am going to limit the discussion so that you can see how all the pieces of this happiness jigsaw fit together. Mind you, I don't think that relationships are essential to happiness, but a good relationship can definitely help us to feel happy. The key here is to find the balance between our individual needs and the needs of the relationship. In a good relationship, both people have the space to grow as individuals as well as a couple.

Let's have a think for a moment about relationships. What does a good relationship mean to you? When you make the decision to enter into a relationship with someone, it is not just you and that other person who come to the party. You each bring with you your values, beliefs, self-talk, stories, traumas and development from early childhood. That's why it is important to avoid placing expectations on your partner or on a situation which is affected by so many factors. To allow your happiness to be determined by another person who has their own story is simply another way of giving your power away. Your ideas of what constitutes a quality relationship, your perspective, your self-awareness and your goals are likely to vary from your partner's. And all of this comes together through the commitment that you decide to set.

A commitment is a pledge or a promise you have to yourself or to someone else. The commitment we have in a relationship involves an interplay between the relationship we make to the other person while simultaneously honouring the relationship we have with ourselves. My dad always said that there are three commitments in every relationship. There is the one you have to yourself, the one you have to your partner, and the one you have to the relationship. I guess this is part of the reason why he is still in love with my mother after over fifty years of marriage. As he says, "Honour each commitment in its own right and give it the space to grow." This involves being able to:

- **Accept change**. All relationships involve change. Once we accept change, we let go of the need to control and expect. Try to take the 'shoulds' and 'musts' out of your relationship and allow change to happen.

- **Let go**. When we let go, we release and cleanse ourselves of emotional baggage, thus giving us the freedom to be ourselves.

- **Require change.** This means asserting and being yourself, which can happen when we lay boundaries and limitations in the relationship. Once we assert ourselves, we draw a the line in the sand to protect our sense of self and enact our self-respect.

Your understanding of a relationship and the agreements within that relationship are likely to be different to your partner's understanding. The inevitable result of this will be an occasional disagreement. It is not the disagreement which matters so much, because all good relationships have conflict. Rather, it is your manner of conflict resolution. It is the commitment you have towards yourself, your partner and your relationship, along your levels of resilience, that matter.

Take some time to define the commitment you have with yourself and the one you have or would like to have with a significant other. What values are involved here? Do you or would you honour these values? How do you balance the needs of the relationship with your own needs? Are the values you choose in your relationship with yourself the same or different to the values you in your relationship with your partner? Once you have reflected on your understanding of commitment, let us look at how to set boundaries to maintain your sense of self and honour these commitments with integrity.

Boundaries

A feature of a healthy sense of self is the way we understand and work with boundaries. Personal boundaries are the limits we set in relationships that allow us to protect ourselves. Boundaries allow us to maintain a sense of self. They are not about locking others out, but rather about being aware of who you are and where your limits lie. I know that as a younger person, I was a little wary of setting boundaries as I thought I might lose friends. We may be reluctant to set boundaries because we lack a sense of self worth. Other reasons we may fear setting boundaries include:

Chapter 3

- we want to be liked
- we are afraid the dynamics of the relationship may shift
- we lack self-awareness
- we fear conflict, rejection or the disapproval of others.

Boundaries come from having a good sense of our own self worth. They make it possible for us to separate our own thoughts and feelings from those of others, and to take responsibility for what we think, feel and do. Boundaries allow us to rejoice in our own uniqueness. They let us get close to others when it is appropriate, but enable us maintain our distance when we might be harmed. Good boundaries protect us from abuse and pave the way to achieve true intimacy. They help us take care of ourselves. To set assess your boundaries, ask yourself these three questions.

1. Does a particular action you or someone else takes, or the values or beliefs you or someone else hold, allow you to be yourself?
2. Does the action you or someone else takes, or the values or beliefs you hold demonstrate consistent kindness, respect and compassion?
3. Does the action you or someone else takes, or the values or beliefs you hold support and encourage your physical and emotional wellbeing?

If the answer is no to any of these questions, you may lack good boundaries. You may want to write a couple of paragraphs in your journal reflecting upon these questions.

Exercise 4: Learning to say no and setting boundaries

I designed this exercise after reflecting on my own history of needing to please and how this at times has impinged on my freedom to be myself. In this exercise, we look at setting boundaries in order to allow the space to be ourselves and to grow as compassionate individuals with potential and possibility. This exercise is in three parts. The first involves practicing being assertive and saying no. The second is about setting boundaries and dealing with conflict, and the third focuses on feeling compassion and letting go.

I would like you to keep at front of mind that we have three choices with all relationship issues. These are to accept, change or withdraw from a situation. I love that Albert Einstein quote about the definition of insanity is doing the same thing over and over again and expecting different results. Rather than be a victim and allow another person's unacceptable behaviour to breach your boundaries, it is more empowering to attempt to change the situation where feasible, but also to know the time to accept and withdraw with respect and compassion.

Part 1: Learning to saying no

Do you ever feel exhausted and crowded because you feel you can't say no? Or perhaps you get frustrated because you feel at times that you have been disrespected? A part of being self-aware is creating the space to be yourself by simply saying no. I am not talking about shouting NO or reacting fiercely. I am talking about the ability to gently but firmly just say no. As I came towards the end of writing this book, I realised that the only way I was going to finish it was to do exactly that and say no. This was hard to do, as I'm sure you can understand, because I like to be seen as the helper. In fact, I'd like to help almost anyone. From a homeless person in the street, to my friends (who are always so good to me!), to my children and their friends... I would help whoever I could. But in the end, all this helping was actually stopping me from being myself and being happy, so I learned to say no. (Or, rather, I am still learning. I need constant practice at this.) It is the ability to say no that enables us to take back control over our own happiness.

In the first part of this exercise, we will set boundaries and practice saying no. When we practice by saying no to little things, we can over time build up to saying no to bigger things. Imagine a small issue which causes you frustration, such as agreeing to do something you are not comfortable doing. Start by saying no, quietly but firmly, to yourself five times in the mirror. Remember the key here is to be gentle. This is not about being rude or abrasive to yourself or others. It is just about establishing boundaries. The trick is to say no to the issue clearly, but without explaining, justifying or rationalising your response. Practice by thinking of five issues in which you feel conflict or frustration. For each of these, say no into the mirror. I suggest you start with small issues. After all, we learn to crawl before we walk.

Some examples that I might look into the mirror and say are:

- *No, I will not look after your children.* (Because I work from home and look after my own kids, the assumption my peers make at times is that I am able to care for their children too.)
- *No, I will not buy you another Playstation 4 game.* (My children feel that if they continue to ask me, much like a broken record, they will wear me down and I will end up purchasing them additional games.)

- *No, it is not acceptable for you to say shut up or use other abusive language.* (The phrase 'shut up' is well used in Australia across a number of social circles, but I consider it abusive and controlling.)

Remember at this stage it is not about finding a resolution to the issue, and it is certainly not about defending your assertion. You are simply practicing the word and the sentiment of 'no'. Notice the tone of your voice and your attitude. Also notice your body language. Are you standing tall with you head up high and your shoulders down? Are your arms open? Look into the mirror and believe in yourself. It is ok to say no. After you have finished this part of the exercise, write about your feelings in your journal. How did it feel to say no? What did you notice about yourself?

Part 2: Setting and maintaining boundaries

In this second part of the exercise, we explore boundaries. What is a boundary for you? Violence, verbal abuse and not being true to one's word are all unacceptable behaviours which definitely require strong, or what I call 'hard', boundaries, but you may also have softer boundaries in place. For example, I do not allow my children to enter the bathroom when I am getting ready (even though they still do at times), or eat away from the table. Nor do I allow them to talk all at the same time (and this one, too, is hard to maintain). What are some of your softer boundaries? What are some of your harder ones? With relationships for me, fidelity and reliability are crucial boundaries.

How do you know when your boundaries are being crossed? When someone acts in a way which makes you feel physically crowded, intimidated or resentful, that is usually a sign that your boundaries are being threatened. Learn how to identify the signs and observe your feelings when your boundaries are broken. We need boundaries for physical health, emotional space, and in order to be self-aware. We have boundaries for protection, security, and to create order and predictability in our lives. Boundaries also help to define and maintain our sense of self and empower us to decide how we would like to be treated by others. How do you feel physically when your boundaries are being infringed upon? How do you feel emotionally? Think of a time when someone crossed your boundaries or imagine a scenario when someone might. What does it feel like? Write it down in your journal.

Now take some time to identify your boundaries and reflect on them. Using the table below, sort your boundaries into 'hard' and 'soft' categories. Then try to identify the values you are upholding with each boundary and make a few notes to explain how maintaining each boundary helps you to feel happy.

Hard boundaries	Soft boundaries	Values involved	How this helps me feel happy

If you are having a tough time standing up for yourself, it often comes back to your sense of self worth. Understanding your boundaries and knowing why you have chosen them can help you define and protect your sense of worth. The answer is practice and being clear about why you chose your boundaries. It may help if you add a few notes in your journal about your reasons for selecting your boundaries and what you will to maintain them.

As with any new skill, please start with baby steps as you practice setting and keeping your boundaries. Don't forget to congratulate yourself for each little step you take forward. Recognise that managing your boundaries is a learning process, so you are not always going to get it right. When you slip up, forgive yourself and continue with your boundary practice. Recognise the value of your boundaries in protecting and affirming you. Learn to say no and have a support system in place as you recognise and work with your feelings around boundaries.

Part 3: Feeling compassion while maintaining your boundaries

Remember your three choices with all relationship issues? They are to accept, change or withdraw. You cannot control or change another person, so you must instead work with what you can control, which is of course yourself. Reflect on this positively as an opportunity rather than a judgement. If you have strong negative feelings, keep in mind that they are yours and not the responsibility of your partner or friend. Deal with the feelings through writing them down and burning or throwing them away, or use your ability to reflect to make a decision on them. At the end of the process, whatever outcome you choose, consciously feel compassion, empathy and love for your partner or friend.

Boundaries are there to protect our sense of self but not to shut others out. That is why our understanding of boundaries always needs to include a focus upon compassion. To help you find compassion even when you may have strong feelings about another person, make a list of everything you appreciate, are grateful for, and enjoy about that person. This does not only need to be about a partner. A friend or even a colleague is fine. Don't stop writing your list until you can feel a sense of compassion towards them, but do keep in mind your hard boundaries or deal breakers, as they are often referred to. These are usually about issues which are more serious and non-negotiable, like verbal abuse, theft or violence. We will finish off this exercise with a nice, comforting boundary meditation.

White light boundary meditation

Sit with a straight back take a few deep breaths. Visualise your boundaries as a white, impenetrable force-field all around you, giving you a margin of clear space between your sense of self and the outside world. Think of this force-field as being like a big dome that keeps you safe and peaceful. Visualise it in detail. See it and feel it covering you, almost like a white blanket that extends out into a dome shape. Within this shape, the white light keeps you feeling warm and cosy. Feel the sense of security and clarity that this white force-field gives you. As you focus upon this sense of serenity, incorporate a sense of feeling compassion for others.

Notice the white light and acknowledge its value. The light is a metaphor for the importance and protective power of your boundaries. Remember that these boundaries help preserve your integrity. They are essential to happiness and they help maintain good relationships. I love to use this exercise to remind myself that in order to feel compassion and care for others, I need to keep my boundaries firmly in place.

What value did you find in this exercise?

My response: I found these exercise to be incredibly useful as they acted as a reminder that I need good boundaries to protect my sense of self. Happiness is simply not possible if I do not define and protect the integrity of who I am.

Your response:

_____
_____
_____
_____
_____
_____
_____

What did you learn from this exercise?

My response: I enjoyed having the three choices in relationship issues to change, accept or withdraw. I found that this reinforced my sense of self and my boundaries. It also alerted me to the fact that I continued to accept a situation which conflicted with my values, making me aware that I needed to strengthen my boundaries. My friend Tara taught me about the white light metaphor and now I use this regularly to protect myself and reinforce my self-awareness.

CHAPTER 3

Your response:

_____
_____
_____
_____
_____
_____
_____

Making space for rituals

I hope you are beginning to see some ways in which you can create more physical, mindful and social space in your life. Not only do I believe that this in itself will increase your happiness, but it will also give you more room to bring rituals into your daily routine. A lot of the significance that rituals have for your happiness lies in the meaning you choose to give them and the feelings that they proffer. This is all about learning to observe your thoughts, your experiences and your feelings so you can train your mind to feel the positive, to remember with joy, to focus upon healthy patterns, and to rejoice in life's small moments. The ritual itself is not the key here, but rather how you explore, practice and observe it, and how your thoughts, behaviours and responses change as a result of regularly performing it.

Rituals are especially effective when they are repeated systematically in the same way and the same space over a period of time. What we are aiming for here is to keep repeating the ritual until it no longer requires any deliberate thought or cognitive load, but simply becomes part of who we and what we do. This gives our minds the space to focus upon living and giving. But what is important is that we don't lose sight of the reason and meaning behind our rituals. This is the bit that matters, and we will learn more about this in the next chapter. What I want to do now is get you started with your third ritual. I think you're going to like this one.

Your third ritual: Using your happy space

This ritual is really simple and really enjoyable. All you need to do is spend time in your happy space. That's it. Just devote some time each day or each week to being in that space. You might like to combine this ritual with some of the other practices you have begun doing, such as meditating or journaling or visualisation. Or you may just sit quietly in your space, perhaps sipping a cup of tea.

If you wish, you can devise some kind of process for entering and leaving your happy space. You might light a candle, say a brief prayer or affirmation, or use a brush to sweep away negative thoughts. Here is an example of an affirmation you may use when entering your happy place:

I enter my happy place.

Here I can be myself.

Here I feel peace and calm.

I let go the past.

I let in the present.

Then take in and release ten deep breaths. This is your space remember, and it is your ritual, so it is up to you to choose what you want to do.

In a nutshell

As I said at the start, this is one of my favourite chapters. There's so much practical information for you here. When combined with everything you've learned in the previous chapters, this idea of creating physical, mindful and social space really sets you up well to start developing your own rituals for happiness. But before we get onto that, here is a recap of the essential messages in this chapter.

- Creating space is not just about letting go of stuff. It is also about letting good things in.
- Editing and decluttering your life and possessions are two great ways to create physical space.
- Our bodies are physical spaces too. We need to think about the physical space within us as well as the physical space around us.
- We can use symbols as visual reminders of our happiness and place these in a specially created happy space.
- There are many behaviours and activities that can help you find mindful space and bring you happiness, including meditation, journaling, realistic optimism and visualisation.
- Personal boundaries are the limits we set in relationships that allow us to protect ourselves and be ourselves. It is ok to set these limits and to maintain them.
- Happiness comes from the space we create physically, mindfully and socially, and from the rituals we practice in these spaces.

Our next chapter really gets into the core idea of this book. It focuses on how you can develop your own rituals for happiness, so make sure you give yourself lots of space to do this. As Graham Hill (2011) says, "Maybe, just maybe, less may be more. So let's make room for the good stuff."

Chapter 4
Develop your rituals

WE HAVE NOW reached the heart of this book. I'm excited because this is the part where you will bring together everything you have learned so far and begin to develop your own rituals for happiness. As we have discovered, a ritual is simply any repeated pattern of behaviour that has a clear meaning and is backed up by values and beliefs. Every ritual has a *purpose*, such as expressing gratitude, celebrating some success, appreciating a relationship, letting go of grief, or simply savouring the moment. A ritual also has a *way of expressing* this purpose, which involves the deliberate, thematic use of symbols, space and time. Rituals differ from habits and routines in that they are designed to enhance our sense of self or community. They may also have additional cultural, religious or social significance.

In Chapter Two, we talked about values which are standards or qualities that we hold in high regard. Our values reflect who we are and what matters to us. The rituals we develop reflect and reinforce our values. In this chapter, we will explore rituals and how they demonstrate our values and enhance our sense of self. There are so many affirming, rewarding and comforting rituals in my life that it is hard to know which one to talk about first. I feel like I have been asked to choose one chocolate from a box full of my favourites. That is why I have decided to give you a snapshot of the different rituals I use throughout my day. I want to share with you how I use these rituals to lift myself into happiness each day and at night too.

Rituals for happiness throughout my day

Six days per week, I wake up around 4.30 a.m. It is one of my core values to be an early riser. I tell myself my own version of the well-known saying *Early to bed, early to rise, makes a woman happy, healthy and wise.* I set two alarms: my Fitbit silent alarm and my iPhone alarm. I like to use an alarm with nature sounds like birds, water or crickets so that I start my day gradually, relaxed and immediately connected with nature. The moment I wake up, I start to notice. Like a mouse that sniffs the scent of a delicious, fragrant piece of cheese, I notice the gifts around me as I awake and I notice too that I have awareness of my existence. I notice my sensual awareness, my sight, my hearing and my senses of smell, taste and touch. This skill of noticing, which is integral to my happiness, is a habit I have only started to develop over the last several years. As I have become more conscious of the value of noticing, I have honed and refined my practice of it. I notice that I am still breathing. I notice my breath and the warmth of my bed. I notice my cosy doona and the glorious comfort of my room. I then think about the millions of people who do not have what I have and I pray for them.

Noticing my morning

I sit up and notice the action of placing my feet upon the floor. First my left foot and then my right foot rest upon the faded but comforting warm wool pile of the carpet. I really notice what it is like to have the texture of the carpet against my bare skin and how much I really enjoy being in my room. I spend several minutes feeling grateful. I focus upon and contemplate the life gifts I feel grateful for. I name them and I visualise them in every detail. I really sit in the experience. This is an important part of my day, because my mood and attitude as I awake set me up for the entire day. It is important that I take ownership of my mood and choose how to direct and shape my mindset. It is the act of choosing where to focus my mind and knowing that it is ultimately my choice to do this which sets the tone of my day. It also helps me see life from other people's point of view, as the feeling of gratitude is like your mind reaching out into the world. When I stand from my bed, I marvel at the cooperative action of so many muscles working together. And then, as I take my first steps of the morning, I feel grateful for the miraculous action of walking.

Essential oils

I light essential oils every morning and evening. I usually use orange, lavender and frankincense oils upstairs in my bedroom, and lemongrass in the kitchen. At times I may use other oils for various therapeutic use. As Helen Keller said: "Smell is a potent wizard that transports us across thousands of miles and all the years we have lived." There is something about essential oils which brings me into the present. I find them calming and centring. Sometimes I place a few drops of lavender oil on my pillow or bed sheets and I do the same for my children. I have chosen my preferred oils because of their supposed effects upon awareness, intuition, happiness and sleep.

Morning workout

In the kitchen, I have a cup of strong tea in my favourite teacup and go to meet with my good friend Victoria for our daily 5am workout. This ritual is about my wellbeing and helps with grounding myself at the outset of my day. My friend and I train together for 60-90 minutes, either doing weight training or walking, depending upon our schedule. It is tiring but exhilarating. Sometimes we walk our dogs at this time. It is a beautiful time of day, still dark and so quiet. We can see the city lights shining as we walk. It is lovely to have time with the dogs as well. I feel very grateful for my friendship with Victoria and grateful for my physical activity too. Something about working my muscles and taking my joints through their range of movement releases endorphins which contribute to my state of happiness. On days when I feel a little concerned about an issue in my life, I find the training lifts my mood. I am a big believer in increasing happy endorphins through exercise. It's true that I find getting up at 4.30 a.m. really, really hard, but meeting a friend makes me accountable and it sets me up for happiness throughout my day.

School run

I finish training at around 6.15 a.m. and then wake the kids. The school run is particularly challenging, as my kids are young and not yet independent. There are always conflicting dynamics and children at that age struggle to complete tasks or manage time with any real discipline. I am constantly herding them, much like a shepherd. Often I have a talk with myself after dropping the kids off at school. I must be a sight for passersby as I sit counselling myself in the front seat of the car after the morning's mayhem. Generally, I look at the positives of the situation and focus upon what was done well.

Breakfast

Breakfast is another big part of setting up my day. I have breakfast after the school run so that I can sit in quiet to enjoy it without distraction. Before breakfast, I light my candles at my altar. I created this altar to give me comfort. I also burn my oils. I will mention this ritual later as a really important practice for supporting my resilience and self-awareness. For breakfast, I have either porridge with two egg whites stirred in and cooked with the oats, or I have poached eggs with spinach. I add raw organic flaxseed oil to both of these. As I eat, I feel very grateful. I focus on enjoying each bite. I ensure that there are minimal distractions so I can eat fairly slowly and really experience eating. I enjoy my view out to my garden and the natural morning light coming in from the window. I ritually repeat these patterns of behaviour to train my mind to be directed towards the positive and to reinforce my self-awareness.

Gratitude practice

This includes using my ritual of feeling grateful as I brush my teeth. This is something I do at least twice per day, so it gives me ample time to reflect upon what I have. As I brush, I name and visualise the gifts in my life for which I feel grateful. I find the hypnotic, repetitive circular motion of brushing my teeth helps with drawing me into a meditative, grateful state. Sometimes I simply repeat the words 'thank you' in my mind and associate this with the repetitive action of brushing.

Associating a specific mental state with a physical state like this can help train our mindset. This ritual of thinking and feeling gratitude is now automatic for me when brushing my teeth.

Meditation

Meditation is a big part of my day. I find it challenging to set a lot of time aside for meditating, so I use small pockets of times throughout the day. Sometimes I meditate while on the treadmill or when waiting for the kettle to boil. I even do it when waiting in line at the shops. Meditation requires a level of inner focus, so I don't do it while driving or engaged in other tasks that require my full concentration. Selecting sustainable rituals is important. It is always better to do a ritual for a shorter period every day rather than a longer period less frequently.

Exercise

I do weight training twice on most days. The second session is a short twenty minutes, which I generally do before I collect the kids from school. I do this session as a little gift of space to myself, to clear my head before the evening. Perhaps you are different, but I found that I only started to feel fully aware of who I am when I started to exercise. Exercise quietens my mind and gives me the space to reflect, be silent and detach myself from the day. I also found that exercise helped me feel comfortable with my physical self and gave me perspective to let go of the trivial issues of life. Once I started to exercise, I never looked back. I have always been that way.

My journal

I set aside at least ten minutes per day in the morning and again in the evening to complete my journal. This time is so precious to me. I like to make the amount of time for journal writing realistic, so it is an achievable ritual. I cover the following areas in my journal, in no particular order:

- fitness and wellbeing
- short-term and long-term goals
- values and beliefs
- review and reflection
- celebration and reward
- gratitude and compassion.

Videos and podcasts

As I was writing the last stages of this book, I found I needed to put aside a lot of what I routinely do. It was hard for me to put aside some of the rituals which give me pleasure and comfort, but I knew the book was important. Usually, I try to produce at least two YouTube videos per week. These are about meditation, yoga and my personal reflections. I also create a podcast called 'Being Well with Lauren'. I really enjoy creating these videos and podcasts. Doing so has become part of who I am. In spite of my best endeavours, my role as a mother means at times I may take a week off creating videos to manage my children's needs. My rituals have helped give me the self-awareness to teach me that there are times to let go of a routine.

Decluttering

Another thing I do every day is cleaning and decluttering. Although decluttering makes me feel good, as a mum of four young children who each has their own pursuits including basketball, singing, guitar and homework, I find it challenging to find the time to clean, and so I ritualise it. By this I mean that I diarise or set time aside for decluttering and cleaning, and I give this time and activity meaning. Each morning, I decide on three decluttering tasks I will achieve each day and I add them to my diary. When done, I tick these off and feel good as I achieve them. The ritual component of decluttering includes setting the task, achieving it and consciously feeling good for doing so. Perhaps the task may be tidying the shoe cupboard (a job which is never finished, by the way) or going through and sorting my papers. Or it can be as minor as rearranging one shelf.

With four children, it is simply not possible to do everything but I know how important it is to always feel a sense of achievement. I journal about my progress and journal about the reasons why decluttering means so much to me. In the last chapter, I wrote about creating emotional space through decluttering. Decluttering and cleaning are not just about the physical acts. They are representative of cleaning and decluttering your mind in order to create space for self-reflection, meditation and a sense of self. Decluttering clears the mind of emotional cobwebs. Sometimes we hold onto physical items because we are afraid or reluctant to let go of emotional memories. This means that when we declutter, we may sometimes find that we can let go of the emotional attachments too and thereby we feel empowered and directional. As this book has taken the best part of 15 months to produce, and I have had a great deal of trouble finding the time to write, some of my regular duties have needed to be placed on the backburner.

Regardless of this, I still schedule decluttering time, as it gives me a break from writing and it makes me feel good.

My tea rituals and podcast ritual

Producing my podcast 'Being well With Lauren' is a vital ritual that gives me so much enjoyment and satisfaction. After breakfast, I make a cup of tea and sit in my favourite chair by the window to record an episode. These episodes have the theme of wellbeing but they are delivered as if I am talking to a friend, so I sit and sip my cup of tea as I talk. This is a treasured time for me, as the light of the morning sun streams through my window and I feel just as if I am having a cup of tea with a close friend and having a heart-to-heart chat. I find the experience intimate and comforting. Towards the last few months of writing this book, it was difficult to produce regular podcast shows as the book required my concentrated effort. Once again, I was kind to myself about this and understood that there are times when we need to embrace change in order to achieve a goal.

Drinking tea

You will have noticed by now that many of my rituals include drinking tea. Having a cup of tea by myself or with others is a vital daily ritual for me, as I find it can be comforting, engaging, and rewarding. I want to talk for a moment about the symbolism for me of this ritual. Using a special pot and cup make the practice meaningful, and the process of steeping the tea gives me time to move slowly, concentrate and just breathe. This ritual can be done alone or with others. It can symbolise friendship or solitude. Waiting for the jug to boil and the tea to steep, smelling the aroma of the tea, feeling the texture of the cup, and taking the time to sit and sip are all so profoundly comforting to me. The physical act of swallowing the tea also allows me time to slow down and contemplate. My senses of touch and taste are engaged and I just love the various aromas of tea. Sometimes I might add a slice of lemon to my tea. I enjoy inhaling the aroma of the lemon as I cut a slice for the cup. My favourite tea blends are English breakfast, peppermint, green, detox and liver cleanse. It is important for me to have symbolism around drinking tea. The choice of cup, brand of tea and a particular air of ceremony all play an important role. Drinking tea allows us the time to catch our breath and physically slow down. I find it interesting that one cannot drink a cup of tea when feeling stressed. You need to relax your throat and the linings of the throat first, and I believe that the act of relaxing our throat affects our whole body. It helps us to breathe, to centre and to let go.

Yoga

Yoga is a big part of my life. Although I have practiced yoga for years, I only started to take it more seriously towards the end of my marriage. The concentration that the poses required, the flow of the movements and the mobility required helped me to feel calm and centred. Now yoga is a way of life. Each day I do eight minutes of yoga and at times I attend a class if I feel like having a little more structure. I understand that this is not much. I would like to do more meditation and yoga than this, but I find the commitment of eight minutes easy to achieve and easy to maintain. Every day I do several sun salutations to greet the day, open up my spine and regulate my breathing patterns. A sun salutation is an excellent way to revitalise and it strengthens and stretches all the muscles. There are several ways to do a sun salutation, so it is important to choose one that is achievable and safe for you. As with all exercise programs, it is a good idea to talk to a doctor before starting a sun salutation practice. I would also suggest you learn how to do the practice through a yoga teacher before attempting on your own.

Tadasana (mountain pose)

I always start and finish my sun salutations by standing in *tadasana*. This is the Sanskrit name for 'mountain pose'. This pose in its basic form (and there is more to it than this) involves standing with the feet almost together, arms straight by the sides of the body, palms facing forwards, shoulders down, back straight and head lifted. It is the basic pose for all yoga asanas (poses). Mountain pose aids consciousness and self-awareness, and reminds us that we, like mountains, are connected to the earth. Sometimes I just stop in the natural light by the window and spend a couple of minutes basking in the glory of the day in mountain pose. This calms and centres me.

Hip opening and letting go

Hip opening yoga poses are such a big part of my life. Over many years I ran ultra distance events without placing a lot of emphasis on stretching and mobility. Running for hours each day with poor biodynamics slowly started to damage and erode my hip joints. At this time, I also lacked a sense of self and worried about what people felt about me. I would run long distances to help me think, but really, I was running away from myself rather than taking the time to look within. Then when I fell pregnant with the twins, they displaced my hips and I spent time in a wheelchair and using a walking stick. I now need a hip replacement. At times I am in significant pain and at other times I am ok. I never resent the pain as I am so incredibly fortunate to have my beautiful twin boys in my life. I had them at a stage of life (aged 41) when I didn't think I would have any more children. The pain in my hips reminds me of the amazing gifts and good fortune in my life.

Yoga keeps my hips mobile and allows me to delay the operation. Hip opening poses also help to protect the spine. In yogic traditions, hip openers have a special meaning and can bring a shift in mindful energy. Yogic philosophy believes that our hips store negative emotions and resentment. They can also relate to us looking backwards in time. Tight hips are also symbolic of needing control and feeling insecure. Opening my hips can help me to let go of the past, and feel creative and optimistic. There are so many hip opening poses, but my favourite is the butterfly stretch. I sit on my meditation chair or with my back against the wall. I straighten my back, lower my shoulders, broaden my ribcage and place the soles of my feet together so that my knees fall gently to each side. I always feel a sense of emotional release when I do the butterfly stretch. Sometimes we sit as a family doing the butterfly stretch. My boys use it for basketball and often play on their PlayStation 4 in this pose. I often drink my cup of tea sitting in butterfly pose on my chair, or I combine it with a breathing meditation. It is a lovely practice that you can try too. But remember, please do not to start a yoga practice unless you consult your doctor first.

Plant ritual

My mother and aunt love to spend time in the garden. I think they inherited their love of plants from my dear grandfather, who would spend hours in the garden each day. It is only in recent years that I am starting to understand their love of the garden. It is something about knowing that we cannot exist without plants and that we are all part of the beautiful cycle of life. As a youth, I used to love to hug random trees and as an adult I still have a strong love of the environment. But it has only been in the last year that I have started to cultivate a garden again and it is just wonderful. The smell of the wet earth, the texture of the leaves, the ritual of tending and watering the plants all contribute to a sense of peace and connection with the earth. I have decorated a corner of my bathroom with plants so that I can imagine I am entering a jungle rainforest when I have a shower. The beautiful potted plants help me imagine exotic birdlife flying around my head. My bathroom has become a tropical sanctuary.

Dinner ritual

For our family, everything circulates around our evening meal. If I were to pick one family ritual, it would be dinner together with our family journaling afterwards, as I wrote about in Chapter 1. My own childhood revolved around our Sunday lunches and festive meals. As my dad worked late, we did not have weeknight dinners together as a family, but every weekend we sat together for every meal. These days, as a single parent, I am constantly multitasking and often buzzing around like a blue-bottomed fly. It would be easy for me to neglect having a family dinner, yet this is the ONLY time we can come together to talk, reflect, laugh and share stories. Our dinners really build a sense of who we are in our own right. We ask each other about our day. We listen to each other and I talk about the daily news and the message of the day. This message may be about boundaries, being positive, dealing with bullying, or letting go. I talk a lot about the importance of being a team, cooperation and building a sense of belonging. I really enjoy our sharing, conversation, eye contact and laughter.

Over the years, I have done significant work with homeless and marginalised people and have spent many hours listening to their stories. One of the strongest themes in their tales was always their need to feel that they belonged. They wanted to hear their names spoken and feel that they had value. One of the ways that I have been able to do this is through sharing a meal with them. I always remember doing so, and I feel fortunate when we eat together as a family, as it is so much more meaningful than just eating. It is also about acknowledging each person's worth, affirming that they belong, listening to each other, caring and celebrating. We each have a role in the preparation of the evening meal. My son often likes to make what he calls his 'special salad'. My daughter pours out our drinks of water. We set the table as a family. After dinner we clean up and then write in our journals. We work as a team and I love it.

Extracurricular activities

In my day there are of course the rituals of attending (oh so many!) extracurricular activities. I consider these very important rituals as I have the ability to acknowledge my children's worth, affirm their value and be present as part of a family. I attend school assemblies whenever my children perform. My girls have regular theatre productions. My children and I often go for long walks in national parks which we call 'family treks'. For the children, these rituals are a vital demonstration of family support and togetherness. Through these, they start to develop who they are. I attend basketball several times per week. Over time, I have grown close to other parents involved in these activities and this has become an important part of my support network, although this may not always be possible with people's work schedules. I recently attended a basketball tournament and the communal feeling among the teams' parents of supporting their children, sharing duties of scoring, getting involved in Nerf gun wars and then celebrating afterwards with team photos and a meal of fish and chips is one of my happiest memories.

Friendship ritual

Another important ritual for me is around friendship. When I was younger I was not always consistent in my contact with friends, so now I ritualise my engagement and treasure my friends dearly. I have so many wonderful friendship rituals and to be honest, at times these are my anchor, giving me a sense of support, guidance and an opportunity to laugh with genuinely empathetic wise women. There are the busy family pizza nights with spiritual Tara and her kids, the fast walks with vibrant Anita, and the training with animal-loving Victoria among many others. I look forward to these and find them so comforting. I always feel more directional and aware afterwards. The power of positive friendship is crucial to building a sense of self, but there is one disclaimer I must put here. I have learned through time that it is vital to choose one's friends carefully. I choose my friends because they are honest, positive and compassionate. When I am with people now, I listen to my body. If my breathing is even and my body is relaxed, I trust that this is a positive connection. My mother always used the saying that 'birds of a feather flock together'. She is so right. The friends we mix with help shape us, define us and affirm us.

I have a special story to share with you about the importance of friendship. I have had a romantic dream, or perhaps 'hope' is a better word, which I have shared repeatedly with many of my friends and I recently talked about this on my podcast. I love the tree of life symbol. I love how it represents the cycle of life, the balance of humanity, the environment and eternal life. For me, it represents my journey of self-realisation. My dream was that a future partner would buy me the tree of life symbol as a gift. I fantasised that this would be a significant romantic moment which would signify that I had found 'the one'. You know what I mean, by this. It would tell me that I had found my Prince Charming.

On my recent birthday, two of my dear female friends, Anita and Jan, each bought a tree of life for me. It was a very special day because I had so wished prior to receiving these gifts that a particular man would buy me the tree of life symbol, and yet it was my good friends who gave it to me. And that meant everything to me. These two tree of life symbols sit by my bed to remind me every morning and at night of the true value of predictable, genuine, loyal friendship. During the day, I wear them. It just goes to show happiness is not about the bliss, the love affairs and the passions. It is about always being there, and that constant, reliable human connection of friendship. That is what my two tree of life symbols remind me of each day when I wear them.

Worry box

On nights when I am concerned about an issue, I give myself five minutes to write it down and any possible resolutions to it. The key is not to overthink this but to put the issues to bed, so to speak. Once I have written down my issues, I fold up the paper and place it in my worry box. And then I consciously close the lid. Everyone in my family keeps a worry box and pen by our beds, although my son's worry box is invisible, as he likes to imagine it. The children decorate their boxes, but mine is plain. The kids use this ritual more than I do, as they have greater difficulties with boundaries. I don't use my worry box every night, as I believe it can take my focus unnecessarily to the negative. However, if I feel that something is bothering me, I will write it down and place it in the box. Then I say, "I choose to see this issue in perspective and I choose to close the lid on this issue for today." Then I close the lid.

Gratitude jar

This is a glass jar I keep on the fridge and it is full of cards. On the cards are written caring acts you can do for others. The children and I sat down and wrote on these cards a number of compassionate things that we could do for other family members. We select a family member to receive the caring act and then the children all take in turns dipping into jar to choose a card and then do what the card says for that family member. The cards may say things like:

- Tell the person why you love them
- Spend five minutes cleaning their room
- Give the person a two minute shoulder massage
- Give the person a hug
- Choose to do one of the person's chores.

It just elicits such a rewarding feeling to give to another and this also helps keep our minds focused on one task. At times when we may lose family connection through conflict or misunderstanding, this ritual always succeeds in bringing us together reminding us of the big picture and putting a smile upon our faces

Screen time ritual

I must give a big thank you to my friend Tara for giving me this awesome idea. This ritual has literally changed my life, as I find my kids become so easily addicted to using their screens. These include phones, tablets, iPads, computers, PlayStation 4 and computers. Tara lives close by. During times when I have struggled to work through family dynamics as a single parent, I call her and we put our heads together to come up with ideas on how to parent. Recently when I was struggling to get the children to help or listen, I rang her for support. Tara told me about a great ritual she had started which requires her children to earn screen time through accumulating acts which build cooperation, require listening and involve teamwork. Tara then borrowed my daughter and together they whipped up a multicoloured template for earning screen time. The ritual means the children are required each day to earn their screen time by earning points. Different activities attract different levels of points. Activities include things like remembering chores, with extra points for having initiative or for expressing compassion. The points were recorded and turned into screen time. Of course, points can also be lost for lack of compassion and not doing chores. Of our many rituals, this one has made my life so much easier. Ah, thank you Tara! And thank you to my daughter for helping Tara design the template.

Internet box

Each evening we have an internet box ritual. I find this one quite challenging to achieve (to say the least). The aim is that all internet devices go into a box that is kept in the lounge room. This is simply a box which stores all devices with electronic screens, such as iPads, iPods, phones and laptops. Obviously, the television doesn't go in the box. It is just turned off.

These days, there is so much potential for kids to hide under their doona covers and hop onto the internet without their parents' awareness. Not only does this affect sleep but there are also dangers associated with being on the internet. I want my kids to turn off their devices and their minds and slow down well before bed. I also want to be able to structure internet time, as it takes away from eye contact, conversation and engagement. No internet is permitted in the bedrooms after 8pm at the very latest. This is a challenge to maintain but it is very much worth it.

Compassion ritual

On the occasions that I happen to have some issue with someone, such as a misunderstanding, I spend some time imagining what it feels like to be that person and try to see their point of view. An important part of this ritual is the ability to get into their shoes and really empathise with the hardships they may be experiencing. In order to achieve a sense of empathy, we need to reach that point when we feel understanding. I used this ritual to heal my experience with the abusive teacher many years later, and recently I used it when a driver became impatient with me. If I ever feel that I am right or have a strong sense of being wronged, I turn to this exercise because I believe it is important to give up the need to be found right. I believe happiness comes from understanding others while honouring our own boundaries.

It is important to continue with this exercise until I start to feel sincere empathy for the other person, rather than just attempting or 'trying' to feel empathy. In doing so, I lose the negative feeling of unfairness or being wronged. At times when I feel that my children are being challenging, I try to feel empathy and compassion for their situation. Don't get me wrong, I am not a saint, and sometimes feelings of frustration are hard to let go. But by having a dedicated practice for this, I end up letting go of conflict with a greater understanding of others and feeling peaceful before I sleep.

Prayer

Prayer is also an important ritual for me. It is a part of my parents' culture and part of the way I have been brought up. I have many fond memories of family prayer around the dinner table. Saying that, I would not carry on a tradition unless I believed in its worth. Prayer serves so many purposes apart from reinforcing our faith. It allows us to process our day, helps us observe our actions, and enables us to focus upon a positive frame of mind. It is also very important to nourish the spirit. At night before I sleep, my prayers help me to objectify my day, gain perspective and re-identify with the meaning of my life beyond the small stuff.

Sleep ritual

After dinner is over, we have completed our journaling ritual, basketball practice is finished and homework is put away, then it is time for quiet and sleep. My sleep routine is vital, as it is the time that I let go of the day and prepare to quieten my mind. Sleep is integral to wellbeing and to both mental and physical health. Lack of sleep makes it harder for us to cope with change or make reasonable decisions. And it is definitely harder to feel happy without enough sleep. The children have rituals for sleep too. We all become quieter 60 minutes before bed, but to be honest, this is a struggle with my twin boys. I encourage my children to walk more slowly, move more quietly and calm their minds. I turn off the bright lights and use salt lamps to help settle us. I love the warm ambient glow of Himalayan salt lamps and I love the texture of the salt rock to touch. I often put lavender oil on the children's beds. I like my children to feel comfort before sleep, with cosy pyjamas, warm dressing gowns and comfy slippers. I hug my children. All screens go into the internet box (and yes, of course they do try and sneak them into their bedrooms.) My children brush their teeth, get changed for bed, the girls brush their hair, and they have half an hour of quiet reading (and no, of course the boys aren't automatically quiet).

At times, I work with my children's worry boxes. Sometimes my children may play the personal sleep therapy audio I have created for each of them. Then when they are settled, I brush my teeth with my gratitude ritual. I wash my face. I love the space in my bathroom with the plants. I love my bedroom with its beautiful quilted pillowslips, simple decorations and soft light. I reflect upon the positives of the day. I meditate. I pray and I always smile. No matter how busy the day, when all my children are asleep and I am preparing for sleep myself, I always smile. The next day, I get up and do it all again.

You can see how these rituals bring such happiness and meaning to my life. They give me sensations of comfort, engagement and reward. They connect me to my family and allow me to live my values. Did any of the rituals I described have any special meaning for you? Are there any similar practices you do or any you would like to try? Take some time to write about this in your journal. What thoughts did reading about my day and my rituals prompt in your mind?

CHAPTER 4

Other rituals

In addition to the rituals that I perform daily, there are others that are just as special but which happen less often. Here are some of them.

Hanging out with my dad

I love my dad. Once per week I look after him in Melbourne. Doing so has really opened my eyes. I make him lunch and check that he takes his pills. This gives my mother a well earned chance to leave the house and catch up with her sister or friends. On most occasions, my dad sits in his chair and I sit next to him. He listens to me record my podcast and makes comments. I have learned so much from him: his wise words, his love of my mother, and his profound enjoyment of the little things. Recently I was making him sandwiches. After asking what he would like on his sandwich, he asked me to bring him the jar of jam and a spoon. He then spooned a generous dollop of jam onto his slice of bread and with a wry look said to me, "You are going to need to learn how to make a jam sandwich."

This wonderful ritual of hanging out with Dad started as I was in the last stage of writing the book and is by far one of my favourites. My weekly visits have helped me realise what an amazing man he is and how much he has taught me. I have only recently begun to understand the story of my dad's childhood. I have also learned much about the art of noticing. From my dad's love of generous jam sandwiches, to his joy at the sounds of the birds, to the way he enjoys the natural night streaming in his window, my dad knows how to be happy. I feel so much love for him and know that I am the person I am today because of him. I am grateful for that.

'I am ok' ritual

This ritual is a private one and very personal to me, but I have decided to share it with you. You know that as a child I was bullied. You have also probably picked up by now that I am a little bit different to most people. There have been times as a child and as an adult that I have been called names. I still get affected by these names. When I do, I go through a little ritual which I call my 'I am ok' ritual. I have built an altar in my kitchen. (Remember I mentioned it earlier in this chapter?) This is not a religious altar, but it is one which helps to define me. The altar is simple. It has a couple of statues, oil burners and small lanterns and candle holders that I have collected over time and which hold meaning for me. There are several candles that I use in this ritual and it takes a while to light them. As I light each candle, I breathe and say:

I burn brightly.

I choose to burn brightly.

No one else defines my light.

I light my own life.

I am ok just as I am.

I am ok.

This is a simple ritual but it is very powerful to me. By the time I have lit all the candles and look around, there is so much beautiful light shining upon me. I feel comforted by the repetitious process of lighting my candles and by the beautiful flickering light they create. I feel security in the repetition of the words, together with my slow, regular breathing. This ritual gives me a sense of personal control and empowerment. It reminds me that I define my own reality.

My crisis ritual

This one is easy to do and that is deliberate. It can be done in one minute. Yes, that's right. Only one minute. This ritual is a simple one and needs to be, as it is for moments when life goes pear-shaped and I feel like I need an anchor to ground me. This is also for my occasional mummy meltdown moments. Yes, we all have them don't we? Here's what I do. I sit in my chair with a straight back. It is so important to have an elongated spine to help open up the breathing passages. I take ten breaths through my nose and I have a mantra which I use. As I breathe in I say, "I can do this." As I breathe out I say, "I let go." That's it. This is a really simple ritual but one which has been so helpful. For me, happiness is always linked to the pattern of breath. This ritual centres my mind so that I can think more clearly, build resilience and have perspective.

Life-changing movie nights

Ooh, this is definitely a favourite! Don't you just love a snuggle on the couch with blankets, a bucket of popcorn and a good movie? The idea of this ritual is that the movie is a 'life-changing' one. The kids and I pick a movie with a message about resilience, empathy or compassion, which gives us cause to review and reflect as a family afterwards. The characters are always struggling with a level of adversity and they work towards finding opportunity and strength through their experience. We share our thoughts and learnings afterwards, which is yet another wonderful experience of family belonging and togetherness.

Self-kisses for affirmation

Now this is going to sound a little strange but I believe that it works. When I was much younger, my mum always said when feeling self doubt, give yourself a symbolic kiss on the back of the wrist. I thought she was a little strange at the time, but now it makes so much sense to me. It is important that we remind ourselves of our worth and engage with ourselves. When I talk about the importance of human engagement, I also mean the relationship that we have we ourselves. We need to build on this relationship and keep it strong. We all want a sense of belonging and these little self-kisses are symbolic of being included, valued and nurtured. We can also wrap our arms around ourselves to give a self-hug or literally pat ourselves on the back. At times, I sit in my chair and give myself a big heartfelt hug. I mean, I really am my own best friend, aren't I? Are you your own best friend? Why don't you take a moment right now to give yourself a hug? This ritual that affirms you as being your own best friend leads in nicely to my next topic, which is speaking about communal rituals and rituals we do with others.

Communal rituals for affirmation

We are social animals. That means we can flourish and grow in good company. In their book titled *Happiness: Unlocking the Mysteries of Psychological Wealth*, Ed Diener and Robert Biswas-Diener say that "like food and air, we seem to need social relationships to thrive" (as cited in Achor, 2011, p.189). Yet this may not always be true, for I do believe that we can find happiness without depending upon a lot of social engagement. That said, I also believe that a good relationship with others can be the icing on the cake of our own sense of self. As humans, we instinctively enjoy the structure, predictability and order of reliable friendships.

In 2002, Ed Diener and Martin Seligman, conducted a study at the University of Illinois of the 10% of students who recorded the highest scores on a survey of personal happiness (Wallis, 2005). They found that the students who were very happy and showed the least signs of depression had strong connection to friends and family and a commitment to spending time with them (Wallis, 2005). This would suggest that people who form close bonds and engage positively with others seem to be happier. Such relationships need to be affirmed and nurtured. Our rituals are a vital way of asserting our membership in the community, and of feeling valued and secure. Rituals can also be used to give us a sense of our role in the community, as well as our identity and a sense belonging. They can help us feel happy through affirming both our individual and communal self. This of course relates to the way of being happy through engaging and empathetic relationships.

Rituals can be culturally specific but still relate to bringing together, affirming and expressing value for communal members. Rituals can also be used as a rite of passage. As individuals pass through various stages of their lifespan, as they have achieved landmarks in life, or their roles may change, there are often rituals affirming their membership to the group, awarding their success or acknowledging with reverence the transitions they have made. Examples of affirming rituals are graduations, debutante balls, awards nights, weddings, landmark birthdays like a 21st or 40th, or celebration of a career achievements. Communal rituals offer us the comfort of belonging, the engagement of friendship, and the reward of feeling needed. The formal aspect of being acknowledged in front of our peers can be incredibly empowering for our sense of personal worth.

And there is nothing more meaningful than feeling a strong connection to others.

Other communal rituals may centre around particular times of year. I personally enjoy Christmas at Mum's and also at my aunt's house, especially the rituals of food, festivity, acknowledgement, sharing and preparation. My mum and aunt have such a strong sense of family, and this comes out in the way each of them carefully decorates the table, the meaningful presents they choose, and their focus on the needs of their grandchildren. My aunt collects novel and unique items and trinkets which she places upon the table to reflect the meaning of Christmas. The children love to touch and look at these various statues and toys. My mum lays amazing floral arrangements artistically upon the table with beautiful handwritten place settings. She keeps these from year to year. There is something special about seeing your own name at the head of your place setting. It gives you such a sense of belonging. The meaning and symbolism of these rituals help us to feel part of a family.

What communal rituals do you use and how do they strengthen your values of family, friendship and community? How do they make you feel? In what way do they affirm your worth? How does participating in these communal rituals make you feel? It's time to get out your journal again and get busy writing.

My rituals: Always a work in progress

From everything you've read so far in this chapter, you might get the impression that I've got it all together. I want you to know that this is all still a work in progress. Sometimes I cry and at times I feel lost, but not like I used to. Each day I feel more self-aware and happier than the day before. These days,

CHAPTER 4

thanks to my rituals, there is always a sense of contentment in me and a strong sense of peace. But even now I do find at times that still I overthink, ruminate or worry about other people's opinions. That's when I return to my rituals. I observe myself and realise that this is always about my own lack of self-acceptance. I want you to remember to persist with your rituals. There are times that I have felt like giving up but I believe the ritual you have on that day is the ritual you have on that day. Even though at times it may not be a miracle, it will still provide a level of comfort, engagement and reward. There are days when my cup of tea may be rushed, my gym routine only ten minutes long, or my connection with girlfriends becomes a late night phone call instead of a dedicated appointment. We need to accept life as it is and search out and celebrate the silver linings. Sometimes I use the time spent waiting in line at the shops to breathe and feel grateful. Sometimes I take just a few seconds to focus on my breathing and on being in the moment. And sometimes it is just a heartfelt hug with one of my babies. But always I remember my values, my gifts, my empathy and compassion, and I return myself to happiness.

Advice for creating rituals

As you can see, most of my rituals are just simple practices that help me notice and appreciate my life. You might like to try some of my rituals yourself or you can create your own. I am a highly structured person by nature and I find structure quite comforting. You may wish for less structure in your ritual practice than I have in mine and that is quite ok. Remember this is your journey and they are your rituals. The ones you choose to create need to reflect who you are, what you value and the meaning you have in your life.

The experience of ritual is different for each person, but it is important to come back to the meaning of each ritual and focus on the 'why' behind it. Keep this in the front of your mind when practicing your daily rituals. In other words, keep your rituals relevant and make sure they are based on your values and beliefs. There is the propensity occasionally to neglect the meaning of a ritual and become consumed by its detail instead. Be careful not to do this. For example, some people believe that Christmas is all about receiving wonderful gifts rather than it being about remembering the meaning of family, focusing on those who are without, and enjoying relationships we have. Sure, the gifts are part of the ritual, but they are not the true reason behind it.

Repeating patterns of behaviour can have a powerful effect on us, not only physically but cognitively as well. The important point to bring home here is that through forming particular habits, we can train our minds to feel particular feelings and to become comfortable with these feelings. Over time, these habits can become like a microchip in our minds, turning on our happy software. That is why you need to keep repeating your daily rituals for happiness until they become as comfortable to you as a well worn pair of tracky dacks. (That's Australian for comfy, casual pants, by the way.)

Remember that this is a process and be gentle with yourself. I have started rituals in the past which have not worked for me before discovering a new ritual that works better. When I first started training with Victoria, I said that I would meet with her just once per week, as I found it too hard to meet with her more often than that while juggling the responsibilities of the kids. Very quickly, I realised that by exercising with Victoria each day instead of once per week I became more balanced and healthier and I had a much more positive demeanour. The early rise was worth the gain of so much more happiness. I also find this with meditation. At times I fidget and can't sit still and wonder why I even try to meditate, but the cumulative effect of achieving small amounts of meditation each day helps me to feel resilient, peaceful and centred. Sometimes we need to really reflect on our rituals and see that the repetition of what may appear to be a senseless action or behaviour is actually making us a better person. This is because rituals can reinforce our values and our sense of self.

You can carry out rituals by yourself or with others. Both are effective and they can serve different purposes. I find that when I am practicing rituals by myself, I am better able to reflect upon who I am. Often after I have completed a ritual, the sense of peace it instils allows me to engage with others more productively and indeed more compassionately. Alternatively, rituals conducted together with others give me a sense of community. Rituals with others can remind us how to converse. They can offer the joy of listening actively to others and the pleasure of ceremony, as well as the health benefits of engagement, humour and empathy. Prayer and meditation in the presence of others can be an incredibly powerful experience too. There is something about the communion of minds through prayer which has a powerful effect upon our sense of tranquillity.

I want to have a word about family rituals here, as I see them as central to my happiness and I believe that they are central to yours too. In saying this, I want you to remember that the word 'family' can mean whatever you choose it to mean. After my marriage ended, my children made up a lovely ceremony to adopt one of my friends as an aunt and include them as part of our family. A family does not have to be based on biological relations. It can be made up of friends or a support group or whoever you want it to include.

I cannot tell you which rituals will be best for you. Practices like meditation and prayer can help you still your mind in order that you may self-inquire and find answers to these questions, but the only way you can work out which rituals are right for you is by trying them out and observing what happens. The most important advice I can give you is that these rituals are about training your mind to feel more comfortable being happy than being in any other state. Always remember this.

Different types of rituals

There are many different types of rituals and many ways to think about them. If you are like me, you might find it helpful to have a system or structure to categorise your rituals. For instance, you could think about your rituals according to the three ways we can feel happiness: experiences of comfort, experiences of engagement and experiences of accomplishment or reward. I must confess that I tried to group my rituals under these headings, but found this classification too narrow, as so many rituals give me all of these feelings at once.

I don't want your experience of rituals to be limited by my attempt to categorise them, but to help you get started, I have come up with four kinds of ritual that can bring more happiness into your life. As each one of you is a unique, amazing individual, you may find that you identify more strongly with certain types of rituals than with others, and you will probably also devise your own groups and categories. The ones I came up with are:

Gratitude

Compassion, empathy and kindness

Resilience and letting go

Affirmation and belonging.

Happiness through gratitude

If you are grateful, you are not fearful.
—David Steindl-Rast

A professor at the University of California has found that people who focus on gratitude and upon the experience of gratitude have a greater sense of wellbeing and happiness (Emmons, 2007). The values of feeling thankful, appreciative, worthy and acknowledged can motivate us to find happiness through expressing gratitude. Rituals for gratitude can make us feel happy in all three of my key ways. They can give us comfort because gratitude rituals are meaningful, they allow us to focus on a sense of enjoying we have, and really just make us feel good. They also help us engage through giving us a structured process to connect with others with a sense of belonging. When we thank others, we affirm who they are to us and acknowledge the worth of the relationship. And we can experience reward in the form of the wonderful feeling we get when we express our gratitude.

What I have learned – and what I hope you are learning too – is that happiness can be found and that there are always events, relationships, and moments to be grateful for. Now at the end of each day, I ritually count the gifts of that day. Perhaps these gifts may be as small as seeing a butterfly alight upon a flower, or it could be a pleasant conversation I have had with my neighbour. It could be kissing my children goodnight, watching my sons play basketball, listening to them giggle, or having a comforting cup of tea with a dear friend. I identify each gift, name it out loud, acknowledge the pleasure it has brought me, open my arms, and experience the feeling of gratitude.

Rituals for gratitude

I have so many rituals for gratitude. Here are six of my favourites. Perhaps you would like to think of a few of your own and write about these in your journal.

1. **Meditate with a focus on gratitude** to help fine tune your ability to take in your surrounds, reduce distraction and encourage a frame of mind for counting your blessings. As you breathe in through your nose, identify a gift in your life and in your mind say the name of the gift. As you exhale, say "I am grateful". Do this for ten breaths that are connected to ten gifts. On the inhale, identify the gift and on the exhale, feel grateful for that gift. Do this either first thing in the morning or as part of your evening routine so that you may ritualise it.

2. **Take the time to write a letter of gratitude** to someone who is meaningful to you. Keep the letter short to ensure this is achievable. Make a ritual of doing this once every week. It doesn't matter whether you send the letter or not, but I am sure you will make someone's day if you do send it.

3. **At the start or end of each day, name out aloud the gifts of that day.** You may wish to do this in highly ritualised manner front of a burning candle or at the foot of a particular tree in order to give it special significance. Or you might have a more casual approach. Sometimes when my mornings are becoming manic, I make the school lunches and call out the gifts in my life as I go.

4. **Focus on 'noticing' a conscious sense of gratitude** for each gift as you experience it. Be like David Steindl-Rast, who felt grateful for electricity every time he turned on a light, or grateful for water when he turned on a tap. I

do this when I eat an apple. I make a ritual of it. I smell the apple and feel grateful for it. I think about how so many people do not have the opportunity to eat apples. I sit down at the table and I cut up the apple. I listen to the sounds of the cutting and the crunching as I eat and this truly makes it an experience of happiness for me.

5. **Start a gratitude diary** or make a gratitude list in your journal. Commit to writing this at the same time each day. Write down ten things you are grateful for. How do these gifts relate to your values? Write a sentence or two about how that gratitude feels to you both physically and emotionally.

6. **Dedicate one meal per week to gratitude** and create a blessing for that meal. You might like to set an extra place at the table and spend a moment considering the needs of others while appreciating and feeling thankful for what you have. Perhaps each family member could express their gratitude one by one before starting the meal. You may have other ideas for a weekly gratitude ritual like this.

Happiness through compassion, empathy and kindness

If you want others to be happy, practice compassion. If you want to be happy, practice compassion.

—Dalai Lama

Our ability to act with compassion, kindness and empathy comes from our acceptance of ourselves and from our acceptance of others. Through consciously trying to imagine and even visualise how other people feel, and by engaging compassionately with them, we can learn to see ourselves as one small piece in the big puzzle that is humanity. We can find comfort in the feeling of kindness and reward in the expression of generosity to others. We can also learn to develop positive responses to suffering, which is another form of reward. I am not sure that rituals which encourage us to feel compassion for others are always comforting, but they are engaging and definitely rewarding. I have learned that by ritually practicing feelings of compassion and kindness, I was actually able to let go of a lot of emotional baggage and past hurts, because once I can feel compassion for those who have hurt me, not only do the feelings of resentment just melt away, but I feel a sense of understanding for the plight of others.

Rituals for compassion, empathy and kindness

1. **Meditate on these feelings of compassion, empathy or kindness** to help to acknowledge others and realise that we are all part of a bigger picture. When you meditate, try remembering how it felt when someone did something kind for you or when you did something kind for someone else. As you find a sense of stillness, focus on the following sentiments. Feel yourself reaching out to the plight of others as you repeat these words:

    May you be comfortable and peaceful.

    May you feel well.

    May you feel a sense of belonging.

    May you live in stillness.

2. **Take the time to write a letter of forgiveness** to someone who has hurt you. You do not have to condone the behaviour, but try to understand it. This is about feeling compassion, not accepting unacceptable behaviour.

Again, it does not matter whether you send the letter. This is about consciously exploring your feelings of compassion and understanding, and letting go of any hurt or judgement.

3. **At the end of each day name the acts of compassion or kindness** that you have achieved. Name the values which are involved here. As I explained above, I like to use the end of the day to feel empathy for anyone I may have misunderstandings with or those who I have met during the day. I do this in my chair before I go to bed, but perhaps you would like to add your own symbols to this experience and ritualise it in a way that suits you. I find through my practice that not only do I grow in understanding, but I also get a much better sleep because my feelings of compassion quieten my mind. The interesting thing about it is that the mind cannot seem to hold feelings of both compassion and resentment at the same time. This means that if you experience compassion, then resentment ebbs.

4. **Focus on 'noticing' a conscious sense of compassion and kindness** through exploring your curiosity. Consciously ask questions about what matters to the people you meet and actively listen to their answers. This is not about finding solutions to their problems. It is simply listening. Try using the responses "I understand" or "I feel for you". The art of curious compassion is very specialised but it is definitely worth developing. Complaining pushes people away, while curiosity invites them in with open arms. It shows others that you value who they are and you are interested in them. I love having heart-filled, caring curiosity. All environmental and social change, and indeed all good relationships, start

with curiosity. The key here is to ask, listen, acknowledge and practice.

5. **Start a project which focuses upon compassion.** Perhaps you could initiate or join a prayer group or group which supports a foster child in a third world country. You might like to raise money for a charity or perhaps raise awareness for a topical issue such as breast or prostate cancer. And yes, it is possible to ritualise such a project, provided it has meaning that is personal to you and that it allows you to enact your values. It is all about the meaning you give the activity and the ritual demonstration of this meaning. Consider how you could ritualise the operation of your chosen project. Perhaps you could make your attendance and contribution to this group a weekly or monthly ritual? Or maybe the meaningful repetition of a prayer, motto or song which binds the group together offers you that important element of ritual. Even the engagement of like-minded people seeking to achieve similar compassionate goals can be ritualised. There are lots of ways to consciously incorporate ritual components into your project to give it symbolism and meaning, so make sure to include these.

6. **Dedicate one ritual per week to feeling compassion, empathy or kindness.** Every morning I light the candles at my altar and remind myself that I am ok just as I am. If you have an altar, perhaps once per week you could light the candles in honour of the sentiment of compassion. Or perhaps you might perform three kind acts per day without needing anyone to know what you are doing, and then write about these in your journal. Another possibility is that you could create a lovely

ritual around fostering compassionate curiosity. The world is your oyster.

Happiness through resilience and letting go

All the world is full of suffering. It is also full of overcoming.

—Helen Keller

Our ability to act with resilience comes from having perspective and staying in the present. It is when we look back in time that we hold onto resentment. We all experience pain and loss in our lives. You might be feeling it right now. It can be a cliché to say that pain is an opportunity to learn, and it is certainly hard to think like that when things are really bad. But pain does give us the chance to develop resilience, and with resilience comes realistic optimism. It can help us develop skills in problem-solving, perspective and self belief. In our pain and loss, we can engage with others and find calm in the face of adversity. There is no greater eye-opener than the raw pain caused by loss, for it has the capacity to make us re-evaluate our lives and our values. This can in turn encourage us to set new goals. The pain of loss also gives us a place from which we have a greater capacity to feel grateful for what we do have. Resilience allows us to let go, which helps us focus upon what counts and makes space for happiness and. When we let go of baggage, we feel comfort. It is resilience which underpins the sustainability of happiness.

Rituals for resilience and letting go

1. **Meditate focusing on resilience and letting go.** Use a guided imagery meditation to imagine yourself as a proud magnificent lion, a resilient tiger or another powerful animal of your choice. As you meditate, imagine your strength. Then, using your new found breathing skills, say inside your mind:

    I am a tiger (or other animal of your choice).

    I am strong and determined.

    I accept my weaknesses and develop my strengths.

    I let go of the past, embrace the present, and plan towards the future.

    I do not need others to define me.

    I define myself.

    I am a tiger (or animal of your choice).

2. **Take the time to write a letter to yourself describing your strengths** and accepting your weaknesses. Describe how important your strengths are and commend yourself for maintaining these strengths. Acknowledge your weakness and make a commitment to continue to work on these.

3. **Consciously practice eye contact and active listening.** Our eyes are the windows to our soul. Make yourself vulnerable by looking deeply into other's eyes. Wherever possible, and depending upon what is appropriate for the occasion, engage in eye contact and affirming touch, such as a high five, handshake or pat on the shoulder, making sure to maintain eye contact at the same time. Acknowledge your friends and ask them how

they're doing. This simple ritual provides a way to feel safe.

4. **Focus on 'noticing' a conscious sense of being present.** I suggest for this ritual that you spend five minutes per week just sitting in the present. A resilient person does not worry or ruminate about the 'what ifs' of the future, and nor do they look back with resentment in the past. Instead, they sit clearly in the moment. So whatever you are doing, truly do that and experience it at least once per week. Perhaps it might be having a shower or going for a walk or eating an apple. The activity itself doesn't matter, but for five full minutes, be consciously and mindfully present for every single breath, movement and sensation.

5. **Start a project which focuses upon resilience and letting go.** A lovely one to consider here is to commit to a restorative yoga practice for 21 days, or perhaps you might try a different kind of health or fitness plan. When our bodies are physically fit and well, we feel better able to let go and feel resilient. Consider how you may ritualise this project. Perhaps you could open your practice by lighting a candle or some incense? Or maybe you could have a meaningful statement or mantra that you recite at the commencement of each? You could also start your project with a particular behavioural pattern like washing your hands or brushing your body with a soft brush to symbolise cleaning or release.

6. **Dedicate one ritual per week to resilience and letting go.** For this, you might like to create a strength-based mentor group, in which people feel safe supported and secure enough to acknowledge their own worth and the worth of others in the group. Encourage members to name their strengths and discuss their weaknesses.

Encourage everyone in the group to identify and experience their strengths. Focus on what matters and practice ways to minimise the trivial issues of each day.

A quick check in

How are you going with these rituals? There is a lot to take in, isn't there? It's funny, but I had no idea that I employed so many rituals until I started to write them down. I think it helps to write them down so you can see if they are relevant and support your sense of self. Perhaps you would like to take a moment now to brainstorm a few of your own ideas for rituals for gratitude, compassion, empathy, kindness, resilience and letting go? Remember to always relate your rituals clearly back to the values which they demonstrate.

You might notice as you develop your practice that a lot of your gratitude and compassion rituals also build your resilience and help you to let go. When we immerse ourselves in gratitude, empathy and compassion, we no longer need to hold on to the past. Our sense of self-awareness gives us the resilience to accept life as it is and provides us with the courage to walk away when necessary. This encourages us to experience affirmation and belonging, which is the final category of the rituals which I want to share with you.

Happiness through affirmation and belonging

If we have no peace, it is because we have forgotten that we belong to each other.

—Mother Teresa

Our need to have our membership of the community affirmed

and to feel a sense of belonging comes from our instinctive need to be loved and needed. As a social herd animal, we need and enjoy signs that acknowledge or celebrate our communal membership. These make us feel like we have a purpose and we matter. Belonging is the feeling of being part of something where we have a sense of acceptance. It is the feeling of security and comfort that comes from being included and accepted, which enhances our wellbeing. Often we just want to be acknowledged as part of the group.

Birthdays, weddings, graduations and rites of passage rituals all affirm our sense of belonging as members of the community. Communal rituals can help us feel comfort, encourage us to engage positively with others, and can help us feel rewarded. Such rituals may be culturally specific, but they are all are about affirmation and belonging. I have learned that feeling a sense of belonging is integral to our sense of self. We enjoy feeling needed and part of something greater and more meaningful than just ourselves. That is the true spirit of community.

Rituals for affirmation and belonging

1. **Meditate focusing on feelings of affirmation and belonging** by remembering that you belong both to your familial, social, cultural and friendship groups, as well as belonging to yourself. Start off your meditation with some regular breathing through the nose and then reflect on your feelings of affirmation and belonging. Visualise every person on the globe holding hands with warmth, compassion and stillness. Imagine yourself as part of this chain of people holding hands, interacting and drawing together all communities, races and nations as one. Actively smile as you visualise this.

2. **Take the time to write a letter to a group to which you belong,** exploring and describing what it feels like to you to belong to this group. Express your feelings of gratitude and worth. Describe the comfort and security of belonging that you experience through being part of the group. Explore the sense of engagement which comes with belonging, and reflect on group ceremonies you have been part of which have been rewarding. Perhaps you may wish to write about how these ceremonies have affected your life. Work towards finding positive experiences in these reflections.

3. **At the end or start of each day, acknowledge in your mind the groups of which you are a member** and feel a sense of belonging. I prefer to acknowledge this sense of belonging as my day draws to a close. I acknowledge my children and tell them that they are loved, that they belong, and that my life would not be the same without them. They are family, my team. I talk to my children about our sense of being a team and the value of working together and affirming each other. I feel so lucky to have had children later in life and constantly share this with my children.

4. **Focus on 'noticing' a conscious sense of belonging.** You may wish to look at a photo of family or friends for this ritual, or pick an event to reflect upon. I want you to remember the occasion and the feeling of belonging instilled in you by the experience. Recall the feelings, the textures, the sounds and the sights associated with this experience and with your feeling of belonging. What is it like for you to belong? How does it feel to you when others affirm your worth?

5. **Start a project which focuses upon exploring a sense of affirmation and belonging.** Perhaps this could be a

communal or friendship group, or it might even be a family group. This may involve organising a worthwhile event or publicly acknowledging a friend or a friend's achievement. What values would you demonstrate in this ritual? What values and beliefs could you draw upon to help create a sense of belonging? How can you make your project a ritual? One of the keys to ritual is meaningful repetition, so perhaps you could meet with this group on a regular basis, and add some symbolism like holding hands at the beginning while jointly stating a mission. I have a friend who after her marriage ended started a group with her friends. Every year they committed to go away on a girls' weekend to engage in a recreational pursuit which would take them out of their comfort zone. The meaning behind this ritual was to cement their friendship and give these women a sense of empowerment. Can you think of a similar project that would cultivate a sense of affirmation and belonging in your life?

6. **Dedicate one ritual per week to affirmation and belonging.** Perhaps this could be seeing friends, having a get-together or family dinner, holding a cards evening or movie night, or celebrating a friendship or family achievement. As an example, we celebrate the boys' basketball goals over a meal and they reflect upon their achievements in their journals. But remember that rituals aren't just random events. They always involve a purpose, values, meaningful symbols and timing.

Pause for reflection

After reading about all of these rituals and all the wonderful practices you might bring into your lives, I want you to reflect upon your feelings for a moment. There's quite a lot to take in here, so ask yourself how you are going with all of this? Are you feeling calm, reflective, eager, intrigued? Maybe you feel a bit overwhelmed? That's ok. You can take this as slowly as you need to. Keep track of your emotions in your journal and spend time in your happy space. Be gentle with yourself. Then, whenever you are ready, you can begin to choose a few daily rituals for your own happiness.

Exercise 1: Choosing your daily rituals for happiness

This exercise is a bit like brainstorming. All I want you to do is to write down some rituals that you would like to incorporate into your day. You may have been inspired by reading about my rituals or been struck by some of the ideas in the lists above. Just write down now any of the rituals you would like to try. If you're feeling stuck about which rituals to choose, go back and have another look at the values you identified in Chapter 2. Remember that your rituals are an expression of these values. You might also like to revisit the list of activities you currently do which help you to feel happy from Chapter 1. Some of these could become rituals too.

Another way to approach this is to write out a snapshot of your day. You will be practicing your rituals daily, so think about the things you already do every day and see if you can include some kind of ritual with them (like my gratitude ritual when brushing my teeth.) Some ideas for this are:

- Waking ritual

- Tea ritual
- Food ritual
- Friendship ritual
- Self kindness ritual
- Exercise ritual
- Meditation ritual
- Journaling ritual
- Sleep ritual.

As you write your list of possible rituals, keep in mind the three ways of experiencing happiness. Think about how your rituals will help you feel comfort, engagement and reward. You don't have to worry about how to do the rituals just yet. Simply write down any ideas that appeal to you.

What value did you find in this exercise?

My response: *The value of this exercise is by naming my rituals, I can start to identify them, own them, and take responsibility for them.*

Your response:

_____
_____
_____
_____
_____
_____
_____

What did you learn from this exercise?

My response: *I have learned how important it is to plan some sort of schedule for my rituals in order to reflect upon their importance and ensure that I will practice them daily. Identifying these rituals by name is the first step to adopting a practice.*

Your response:

_____
_____
_____
_____
_____
_____
_____

Important elements of rituals

For me, the crucial thing about rituals that makes them different from all other activities we do is the *meaning* behind them. It is the significance that we give to a ritual that makes it contribute so powerfully to our lives. That said, let us consider again the important elements of rituals. This will help you as you start to think more deeply about the rituals you want to perform every day. Each ritual has the following elements:

- Purpose – the reason behind the ritual
- Patterns of behaviour and thought – the actual practice of the ritual
- Symbols – any materials or objects that are used during the ritual
- Space – the place where the ritual will be practiced
- Time – how long it takes to do the ritual and what time of day, week, month or season it takes place
- Repetition and dedication – when and how often the ritual will be performed, together with the commitment to do it in order to ensure that it becomes a natural and valued part of each day.

Having a defined structure for your rituals and doing them with certain objects in certain places at certain times will make it easier for you to develop your practice. This will also underpin the meaning of your rituals. While it may be ok at times to deviate from this structure, make sure you return to the meaning behind your rituals. This is always more significant than the ritual itself. After all, the ritual is really just the outward expression of that meaning. All of the elements outlined above are simply designed to make the process more systematic for you.

Exercise 2: Defining your rituals

Now that you know a bit more about the important elements of a ritual, you can start to define your individual ritual practice. Look back at the list you made in the previous exercise and put a tick or star beside those rituals you would like to begin practicing first. It is a good idea to start slowly, so just choose a few rituals to begin with. There is no point in deciding to do eighteen rituals that take half an hour each and then try to do all of them every single day. You just won't be able to manage that. Instead, be realistic and pick a few rituals that really strike a chord with you. Remember the key here is enjoyment and wellbeing. You won't enjoy your rituals if you have so many that they become a chore. And don't forget that you can always add more rituals later on. Chances are that you will want to do exactly that, once you realise how beneficial your ritual practice will be.

For each of the rituals you have chosen to begin with, write down:

- Purpose (the reason behind the ritual)
- Patterns of behaviour and thought (the actual practice of the ritual)
- Symbols (any materials or objects you need)
- Space (where you practice the ritual)
- Time (how long it will take and the day, week, month or season for it)
- Dedication and repetition (when and how often you will do the ritual).

Consider, too, whether there are any rituals you will perform with other people, and keep in mind any adjustments you may need to make to accommodate their needs as well. Remember, my friends, this doesn't need to be complicated. Many of your rituals can easily be added to your existing daily activities. Finally, for each ritual, write down a few lines about how it will help you feel happy.

What value did you find in this exercise?

My response: *I found this exercise valuable because it helped me to explore the structure of creating rituals and also to notice how this structure supported and reinforced my values. I found it interesting to notice how the structure of a ritual itself can be comforting and reassuring.*

Your response:

_____
_____
_____
_____
_____
_____
_____

What did you learn from this exercise?

My response: *I learned that even though rituals may not obviously support or reinforce happiness, their use of symbolism, timing and space, supported with practice, can help to create cognitive change and literally teach me to feel happy.*

Your response:

_____
_____
_____
_____
_____
_____
_____

Exercise 3: Your daily ritual map

Congratulations! You now have everything you need to create a map of your daily rituals for happiness. We have looked at different types of rituals. We have looked at what makes up a ritual. We have looked at how rituals help us feel happy. Now we are going to design a ritual map. In days gone by I used to be an event planner, and one thing that I have found to be really important is that we map out our lives. From mapping our goals to mapping our thoughts, and on to our patterns of behaviour, mapping helps give us perspective and context so that we can observe our lives with some objectivity rather than be distracted by sitting within them.

It is logical, therefore, that mapping your rituals will help support your practice. This exercise is about getting all that information down on paper so you can keep track of what you want to do. I would like you to clearly mark down the values employed in each ritual too, and whether these rituals relate to the four categories which we have explored earlier in this chapter. Just to remind you again, those categories are:

1. Gratitude

2. Compassion, empathy and kindness
3. Resilience and letting go
4. Affirmation and belonging.

You can use the following template to map out your rituals or perhaps you could design your own. You might like to highlight your most important rituals in some way.

Name of ritual	Time of ritual (when and how often)	Type of ritual	Value which applies	How this makes me happy
Dinner ritual, including preparation, serving, dining and cleaning up, together with journaling	Daily at each dinner time	This ritual covers all four areas of gratitude, compassion, resilience and affirmation	Sense of family, team, cooperation, empathy	I just love listening to my children chattering over a meal and reflecting on their day. I like to listen to them, look into their eyes and hear their stories.

What value did you find in this exercise?

My response: *The value of ritual mapping is that it allows me to clearly match my values with my rituals and it gives me the perspective to keep my rituals relevant and reflective of who I am. I could also see how my rituals help me feel comfort, create opportunities for engagement and encourage a sense of reward.*

Your response:
_____
_____
_____
_____
_____
_____

What did you learn from this exercise?

My response: *Just as a map helps us to navigate our way to the finish line, so we can see more clearly with a ritual map that our rituals support all our values and our life's purpose. I learned that ritual mapping is just like goal mapping in that it can help give us perspective on our happiness practice.*

Your response:

_____
_____
_____
_____
_____
_____
_____

Ritual for reflection and checking in

This chapter has been all about understanding, choosing and creating your rituals. There is just one last thing for you to do, and that is to actually practice them! Your ritual for this chapter is simple. Just make a commitment to check in with yourself at least once a week to see how you are going with your daily rituals for happiness. You could choose to do this in your happy space or you might want to write about it in your journal. Perhaps you could make a template for yourself, so you can keep track of your rituals and take notes on each one. The important thing here is not to judge yourself. You are just starting out, so be patient and compassionate. This is the time when you will learn how to create a sustainable practice of daily rituals. Which ones do you find easy to do? Which ones are harder? Which ones might you need to adjust a little? Set aside time each week to write, reflect or meditate on your daily rituals. That is all you need to do.

In a nutshell

You know what comes next, dear friends. Here is your summary of the essential information in this chapter:

- A ritual is a pattern of behaviour that has a clear meaning and is backed up by values and beliefs.
- Every ritual has a purpose and a way of expressing that purpose, using symbols, space and time.
- I use many rituals throughout my day to enhance my happiness and appreciation.
- Each of us experiences rituals differently, but it is always important to come back to the meaning behind our rituals.
- You may find it helpful to think about your rituals according to certain categories.
- There are lots of examples of daily happiness rituals you can try.
- Every ritual includes the essential elements of purpose, patterns of behaviour and thought, symbols, space, time, and repetition and dedication.
- Mapping out your rituals can help you get perspective on them.
- It is important to check in with yourself regularly to see how you are going with your rituals. This will help you learn what you need to know to make your practice meaningful and sustainable.

And speaking of creating a sustainable practice, that is what we will be learning about in the next chapter.

Chapter 5
Practice daily

CAN YOU BELIEVE we are at Chapter 5 already? What a journey it has been! Before we travel any further, I want you to take your hat off to yourself for getting this far. You have learned so much, worked through the exercises, started practicing your rituals, and have been open to change. As a result, you have taken big steps towards creating your new – and happier – reality. These are major accomplishments, my friends. Believe me when I tell you it is not easy to change. In fact, most people don't change unless they absolutely have to. That is why I want you to really sit in this moment and enjoy that sensation of reward. I am proud of you, so take the time to congratulate yourself. You have done so well.

The reason change is often difficult is because most of us are creatures of habit, but what does that actually mean? We find comfort in repeating particular patterns and behaviours. Repetition makes us feel good. We find it hard to create new ways of thinking, feeling and behaving, and it is harder still to keep going with those new ways, especially when things get tough. This chapter is about ensuring that you are supported in your happiness rituals so you can maintain your practice and sustain it through difficult times. As we all know, life can be full of tough times, especially when we least expect it. Let's explore some practical strategies to help your ritual practice become a happy habit. We will also look at contingency plans, systems to encourage accountability, and how to encourage self-acceptance when everything seems to be going wrong.

You will be discovering for yourselves that rituals are vital to our wellbeing. They enable us to affirm our values, develop positive feelings, connect with our communities and ourselves, and experience genuine happiness every day. In some ways, our rituals are the essence of who we are. We chose them, after all! But even so, there will be times when each of us will face struggles with our rituals. Let me reassure you that this is normal. I could tell you lots of stories about how the challenges of life sometimes place pressure on my ability to keep up with my rituals. I have included some of these stories in this chapter, so you will see that you are not alone and that regardless of whatever else might be happening, you can still find ways to practice and adjust your rituals if necessary. You are the one who designs them. You practice them and you enjoy them. The key message is this: if your rituals are not making you happy, then change them. Your rituals are there to help you. This is so important to learn, so let's get into it.

Making a habit of happiness

Let us start off by thinking about what 'practice' really means. The word itself refers to the customary, habitual or usual way of doing of something. It is about the regular and repeated performance of an activity or behaviour, or the exercising of a skill so that we might acquire, improve or maintain our proficiency in it. That's where the phrase 'practice makes perfect' comes from. We are certainly not aiming at perfection with our happiness rituals, but we are aiming at developing the skill of learning how to feel happy every day.

In order to make sure that we acquire, improve and maintain our ability to feel happy every day, we need to regularly repeat our rituals until they become habitual. Now it might seem like a habit is the opposite of a ritual, but they actually work together. Habits are usually simple, repeated behaviours that lack any real thought behind them, whereas rituals are all about the deeper meaning. We may have a habit of randomly eating over a sink, but a ritual would be setting the table, placing hand picked flowers in a vase as a centrepiece, cooking a friend's favourite dish and sitting together to celebrate that friendship on the first Monday of each month. You can see the difference here, can't you? One is just routine, while the other is an occasion that is full of symbolism and meaning. Yet in order for us to experience happiness, we need to make sure the meaningful occasion happens regularly, and this is why we need to use the techniques of habit formation to maintain our ritual practice.

Habit formation occurs when our patterns of behaviour become automatic and are part of our cognitive framework. The value this has for maintaining our ritual practice is that it allows us to direct our attention towards performing our rituals and remaining aware of the meaning behind them without needing a cognitive prompt to do so. In other words, when we allow our rituals to become habitual, we can still get all the good feelings and mind training that comes from doing them, but without the effort involved in consciously reminding ourselves all the time that we have to do them. By employing the power of habit, our rituals become like an automatic program in our head, while still retaining their precious elements of reverence, devotion and dedication.

CHAPTER 5

The ritual you have

The thing about being a single mum of four young children is that time is continually snatched away from you. It is like being at the top of the Luna Park roller coaster in the Melbourne suburb of St Kilda and looking out at the ocean with the word "amazing" on your lips, just enjoying the incredible view. Then all of a sudden you are plummeting with your stomach leaping into your chest as you roll into a dizzying tumult of ups and downs, lefts and rights, lurching this way and pitching that. Most of us will experience something like this, even if we are not parents. It's called life, I think, and it has a way of knocking us off our path sometimes, no matter how organised or prepared we think we may be.

All the Excel templates in the world could not have prepared me for the surprises, joy and mayhem that my children create in my life. Their needs are often unplanned, demanding and emotionally exhausting, and that is simply the nature of motherhood. While trying to finish this book, I had to deal with one serious school bullying incident, operations for tonsils and adenoids for my two boys (yes, twice), one student drama production that lasted six days, two bouts of gastro, three broken toilets, the shower flooding twice which caused water to come through the ceiling onto the floor below (also twice), visits to the physiotherapist for one of my daughters who has back pain, more visits to the physio and podiatrist for the twins who are growing too fast and have Severs disease, one vet appointment for the cat, stitches for the dog, stitches for the other dog, sleep issues with one child, one jaw operation for my daughter, basketball tryouts, internet problems, and so much more. Yet at the end of each day, I kiss my children good night and feel so grateful, happy and complete.

Throughout these busy and demanding weeks, of course

I still continued daily habits of eating consciously, doing the school run and making lunches. It was all the more important that these habits had a ritual component that had meaning and reminded me of my values, reinforced my positive beliefs and kept me self-aware. What I love about rituals as a mother of four is that they take me out of the manic existence of juggling responsibilities and into the moment of being mindfully present. Every single one of my rituals reinforces and reminds me who I am. This is no easy task, I assure you. Despite my busy (understatement!) life, somehow I still found time to conduct many of my rituals, compromised as they may sometimes have been. It's true that at times I felt like giving up, and I mean *really* giving up. I cried and even (on a very few occasions) walked out of my morning weight training session early. It seemed so ironic that I was writing a book on how to be happy while at the same time ending up in tears.

Then it occurred to me that just like the phrase that an apple a day keeps the doctor away, a meditation a day keeps the sadness away. A daily, achievable meditation ritual is better than a longer meditation practice that happens only every so often. And the same goes for an achievable yoga practice or a family dinner. This always sticks in my head. Like the marathon runner who practices keeping fit, paces himself or herself and maps out the route in order to complete the race, we do our rituals to remind ourselves of who we are, what we hold as meaningful and to celebrate life. To me, part of practicing rituals involves being kind to ourselves, accepting our reality and being grateful for what we have. That is why I say the ritual you have is the ritual you have. At the end of the day, it is much more important to focus on the meaning or reason behind your rituals, rather than worrying about getting every detail of them absolutely right every time.

What this means is that sometimes I exercise by skipping

rope whenever I can over the course of the day or by doing push ups every half hour or so around the house while the kids run around. On days when life is really tough, I may alter my rituals according to my circumstances, but I always still do them, as they give my life such meaning. It is not squeezing push-ups in between family activities which really counts here. What matters is reminding myself why fitness is important to me and affirming the core elements of who I am. For instance, my children and I always make space for our dinner ritual, whatever else is going on, because this is really central to our happiness as a family. Even if this means eye contact and conversation over fish and chips, it is the engagement which counts. Rituals are about demonstrating and reinforcing our core values. As long as I keep my focus on the meaning of the ritual, I can allow myself to be flexible with how I practice it.

Sustaining your rituals through tough times

When I read back over the last edit of this book, I realised that it may appear that my family's life runs like clockwork according to a defined set of well organised rituals. Let me assure you, that is just not true! Our rituals do bring us closer together and help us function as a family, but a lot of the time it feels like we are fighting a series of fires. As soon as one is put out, another seems to ignite. Sometimes I read letters from my readers and viewers who see me as some sort of superhuman guru who always gets it right. Well, let me say here and now that they are wrong. I don't want you to make the mistake of thinking that any of this has been easy. Please, don't ever, ever, ever say to yourself, "Oh, it's fine for Lauren. She is just naturally strong." It is not true. My dear friends, there are no superhuman powers at work here and no miracles either. I have mastered the mummy meltdown, trust me. But I also have the ability – not to mention the necessity – to fall over and get back up again. And again. And again. I believe it is that ability to get back up which truly defines us. And I know that if you have ever fallen down, you too can get back up, my friend.

I know that you have challenges in your life. I know that sometimes things feel so tough and unfair that you have no idea how you will cope. But if you have made it this far and are reading this now, then I know this too: you already have all the resilience you need to sustain yourself and your rituals for happiness through difficult times. You can do it, I promise. You just need a few strategies to help you along the way. Here is my advice:

1. Have a contingency plan
2. Find support
3. Make yourself accountable
4. Learn acceptance
5. Get perspective.

There is so much I want to share with you about all of these points because they truly will help you so much with your practice. Let's start by discussing a plan.

Have a contingency plan

You already know how much I love my Excel spreadsheets. When my twin boys were born prematurely, I already had two daughters aged two and three years old, and I still needed to earn a living. Although I was so excited about having twins, I was also nervous about how I would cope. I made many plans which I posted on my wall. I had all kinds of templates and checklists,

CHAPTER 5

full of ideas and strategies that would help me manage having four children who were all under the age of four. Needless to say, my kids themselves never read these lists and so despite all of my efforts, life still didn't go to plan. But that does not stop me from seeing the value in having contingency plans.

These are plans which allow for all possibilities. They are often used in risk management scenarios to prepare people and organisations for any eventuality that might occur. They are also used in times of war or crisis and are designed to consider any outcome that is different from the one that is usual or expected. This is not about being pessimistic. It is about being prepared. In our lives, contingency plans could be as simple as knowing you can call on someone else to pick the kids up from school when you are running late, or having a phone with you when the car breaks down. You know the old saying that failing to plan is planning to fail? Well, it's like that with our rituals too.

This means that just as we can have contingency plans for day-to-day events, we can also have contingency plans to maintain our rituals. A contingency plan for our rituals will take into account what we might do differently when something happens to change our usual practice. This could happen when we get sick or have to travel or simply find ourselves getting a little bit too stressed and busy. At such times, just when we need it most to help keep us calm and grounded, our happiness practice can be the first thing to fall by the wayside.

My contingency plans for maintaining my rituals involve the following:

1. **Knowing my purpose and values.** My rituals are all about demonstrating my values and creating meaning. When practicing them becomes challenging, I peel the

details back to the bare basics in order to still demonstrate and honour those values.

2. **Identifying and assessing the risks.** By clearly identifying what triggers or issues stop me or hold me back from achieving my rituals, I am better equipped to manage them. Forewarned is forearmed.

3. **Planning for what could happen and having a response ready.** I like to have a planned response for each risk so that I can still maximise the meaning of each ritual, like I did one year with my family when I had no money for Christmas presents.

4. **Prioritising what matters.** In tough times, I decide which are my most important and meaningful rituals and I figure out a way to hold onto these. For example, when life gets tough my weight training sessions become 12-15 minutes daily rather than 60-90 minutes. Because this ritual matters so much to me, I adapt my practice in order that I can still do it every day.

5. **Maintaining my values and being happy.** After all is said and done, practicing my rituals is about reinforcing the values which make me essentially who I am. Even when things are hard, I consciously notice moments of comfort, I make sure I engage meaningfully with others and I allow myself the lovely anticipation of reward. This enables me to be happy.

Break glass in emergency list

Further to having a contingency plan to help manage situations where life goes belly up, I also recommend creating a 'break glass in emergency list'. This list has on it all the things you can do to remind yourself of the value of your practice,

CHAPTER 5

along with strategies to help you get back on track with it. While a contingency plan is designed to help your rituals occur whatever happens in life, a break glass list is a little different. It is for desperate measures and those times in life when you need more of a rescue remedy in order to handle exceptional circumstances. The phrase 'break glass' comes from the metaphor of breaking the glass cabinet in order to get to the axe that you need to smash through the door in an emergency. That's what you need in the times when all else has failed and you are not ready to give up. And believe me, my friends, the foundation of being happy is to never, ever give up.

Being tough and the importance of vulnerability

You know that saying when the going gets tough, the tough get going? Being happy every day certainly requires you to be one tough cookie. There have been so many times when I have picked myself up, one limb at a time, off the floor and just focused on breathing one breath at a time. Then, much like the movie character the Terminator, I get back like a robot to my routine. Of course, this doesn't always work. There was a time during the writing of this book when I became very sick. The doctor suggested, after the fact, that I had non-contagious meningitis. I was in bed, not able to move for several days and could not even lift my head from the pillow for very long.

A couple of girlfriends dropped in to help with driving my kids to school, but by some freak of chance and with everyone being busy with their own lives, no one checked on me directly. My friends would pick up or drop off the kids and put food in the fridge, but for the most part, they did not check upstairs. I probably needed hospitalisation, and yet I kept texting my friends that I was ok when they kindly inquired. I was certainly not ok. When I finally got up three days later, there was little food in the kitchen, the house looked like a bomb had gone off, and I felt extremely weak for days. But rather than being down on myself I just did a little at a time, slowly getting back into my rituals.

Later, a friend said to me, "Don't you see that by not asking for help, you are martyring yourself and you will hinder your progress?" (She was referring to the book.) I thought about this and agreed. I decided that my real fear was that by asking for support and help, I was making myself vulnerable to judgement. I was scared of failing and I was terrified of people judging me for trying. I thought about this and realised that there is resilience to be found in having the guts to be vulnerable. Brené Brown (2013), who at the time of publication presents one of the top ten TED Talks of all time, says: "Vulnerability is basically uncertainty, risk, and emotional exposure" (as cited in Schawbel, 2010). Happiness is a by-product of allowing ourselves to feel and experience life while honouring our values rather than someone else's. So it stands to reason that without making ourselves truly vulnerable, we also forgo the opportunity to be truly happy. And yes, at the time I was unwell, I was just plain scared of exposing myself to any more emotional risk. By not asking for help, I didn't have to worry about being let down or being judged. On the flipside, however, I severely hampered my ability to succeed.

Brené Brown (as cited in Schawbel, 2010) also notes that: "The fear of failing, making mistakes, not meeting people's expectations, and being criticized keeps us outside of the arena where healthy competition and striving unfolds." After this event of falling very ill and not asking for help, my contingency planning became even more important. And it was a good lesson to me that I need to ask for help assertively and clearly if I am serious about being happy. That is why I have a 'break glass' list now.

CHAPTER 5

My break glass list

Coincidentally, as I write this section, I feel so very tired. The shower tap has broken and can't be used. I have too much rubbish to fit in our bin. The lawn has not been mowed. I have issues with the children and I really, really need a holiday. I think about these things, but then I change my attitude and deliberately turn my mind to the positives. I look outside and think how lucky I am. I inhale my lavender oils, enjoy my plants and pour myself a nice cup of tea. I know that it is not always possible to be upbeat and cheery, but our minds are powerful and there is always a degree to which this can happen. With my break glass list, I can just focus on the meaning of my life and my rituals, and allow all else to fall to the wind. Below you will find some of the ways I use this list.

When finding the time to meditate just seems impossible

When I am up to my ears in basketball tournaments, singing lessons, cleaning, taking care of the animals and navigating my children's dynamics, and there is simply no chance for my usual meditation practice, I take ten breaths in through my nose and out through my nose. As I breathe, I lengthen my spine and open my rib cage. You already know that I sometimes meditate in the line at the shopping centre and I also do it while watching my boys play basketball. At times I will go for a six minute walk and meditate as I walk, and of course I dearly love my butterfly pose, so I meditate while doing that for three minutes. When I feel that stress is getting the better of me and I can feel my hips tightening, that butterfly stretch is such a wonderful remedy. Once I ease and lengthen the muscles around my hips, I feel such an emotional release. It is lovely to combine that with a quick meditation. I would like you to remember that meditation is cumulative, like taking vitamins, so it is not about doing a huge one-off meditation, but rather having a little meditate throughout each day. I find every moment I achieve towards quietening my mind helps define me, reinforce my positive beliefs and build my resilience.

When sitting down to dinner gets difficult

I have said many times how important our dinner ritual is to me and to my family, but sometimes after the boys have been to basketball training, we end up just grabbing fish and chips to eat. Even so, we always sit down at the table, turn off the internet, make eye contact and ask each other about our day. Dinner is about experiencing the pleasures of food and the reward of engagement and belonging. A lot of this comes through really connecting with one another. It is when we lean forward from the hips, tilt our head forward and just listen to someone using our eyes that these moments of engagement becomes most powerful.

When life with kids becomes even more hectic

Getting four kids to school is sometimes a manic and stressful ordeal. Don't get me wrong, I just love them, but sometimes I think to myself 'four kids in four years – what was I thinking?' I never forget for a moment how fortunate I am to have these four beautiful children, but their closeness in ages makes life quite busy. Whenever I find myself feeling overwhelmed, I forgive myself and remind myself how incredibly lucky I am. I review with the kids later and we reinforce what it means to be a team and how we can demonstrate our values of family and cooperation. I think it is pivotal for us to always take responsibility for behaviour, whether it is the kids accepting responsibility for their lack of organisation or me for my impatience and frustration. It is important to review situations with the children and even at times to say, "Sorry, I could have done it differently." Kids learn resilience from our vulnerability. I have mornings when the dog steals someone's lunch off the table and runs outside, one child can't find their sport uniform, another can't find their bus pass, and another still can't find their good basketball. These are times to just feel love, accept and let a lot of stuff just go through to the keeper.

When friends are needed to come to the rescue

This is definitely a work in progress, but when life becomes too much of a juggle, I am learning over time to reach out to friends, and boy, do I have great friends! I ring Mum, Tara, Anita, my aunt Denise or Victoria. I cannot put into words the value of my friends now. They have helped me design rituals to assist with parenting, decluttering, wellbeing and loss. Tara has been like a second mum to my kids. Anita has created amazing homemade meals and helped us celebrate birthdays. Victoria has had us over for incredible movie nights. And I cannot count the times that Aunt Denise has come over to help organise our lives and offer love, advice and support. It has taken me a while to understand what true friends are but now my friends are like my family and my mentors. Tara, Anita, Victoria, Mum, Denise, thank you!

When no friends are available to help

Well, first off this is a misnomer. Let's keep in mind that it is not the responsibility of our friends to come to our rescue, it is our responsibility to control our own behaviour, not the behaviour of others, and to ask for help when necessary. If such help is not forthcoming, then we need to think of another strategy.

What we do not do is feel pity, resentment or bitterness when there are bumps in our road. We simply find another way. I am really lucky that my friends are always there for me. And if they can't be there, I know they certainly would like to be. They have their own projects and responsibilities, and their own families, so if they are not able to come and help, I create a virtual friend. That's right, I use my mind to visualise talking to a friend about my situation.

I have said before that our minds are an incredibly powerful tool, and in the end, I am the one who is responsible for myself. So yes, I imagine myself talking to a friend over a cup of tea. After all, it is the support and guidance of our friends which is comforting, and this may be imagined. Of course it is not as good as the real thing, but happiness is about practicing certain feelings, guiding our thoughts, and creating solutions which provide us with comfort, engagement and reward. I know what my friends would say to me in certain situations. If they can't be there for me in person, I can still find comfort in their virtual words. I know that they deeply care for me, so I can focus on the feeling of this care. At times I talk out loud to myself to review a situation with perspective or forgive myself. I know it sounds a little left of centre, but I find that saying it out loud helps give me perspective and insight. Next time you need a friend and no one is available, why don't you try this too? I think you will be surprised how well it works – especially over a nice cup of tea!

When yoga goes express

I love this one. I use an egg timer. Yep, that's right. A three minute egg timer. I was so excited when I purchased it. In fact, I bought four egg timers, one for each child, and we all love them. They have a multitude of uses, and one of these is setting an achievable timeframe on a number of my daily tasks when things start to slip away or crisis looms. I am not saying that we can complete everything that needs to be achieved in three minutes, but when life goes pear-shaped, these trusty egg timers give us an achievable way of structuring a ritual. For instance, when finding the time to complete a yoga practice seems impossible, I use an egg timer and do one or two hip opening poses, then throw in a sun salutation, a mountain pose by my window and a breathing exercise, and hey presto! I feel just a little bit better. And really that is what it is all about. Feeling just a little bit better.

When there is no time to clean or tidy

Nothing substitutes a good clean up, but towards the end of finishing this book, I found that my rituals, including those for cleaning and decluttering, seemed to take a back seat to getting the book done. The concentration and attention to detail the book required meant that I needed to work for several consecutive hours while still balancing the needs of my children. Something had to give. (Well, a lot actually.) I decided to set myself breaks and plan whether I decluttered, went for a walk, took the kids out or watched a movie with them. It was always about reminding myself of the meaning of my life and my family's life. I have clear standards for when life gets tough. As long as the kids are clean and showered, and that the toilet, wet areas and sheets are also clean, I am happy. Of course, I would also check that the children had the comfort of a clean kitchen, a nice bath, a lovingly packed lunch, and a dedicated space to be themselves. And I would always come back to the importance of my values, as they define my present and structure my future.

When a family action list is necessary

This isn't really a break glass list, but it is similar. I used the following family action list to help the kids be a team and cooperate during the writing of the book. This list also served as a bit of a family manifesto and is something we can refer to for a sense of direction in order to bring our minds back to our rituals and their importance in our lives. On those occasions (which were many, by the way) when the children did not do their chores, I would ask them to write a paragraph about what our family values are and we decided as a family to adopt this action plan. I asked them to recognise how important it is that we each practice this plan and what would happen if we didn't stick to it. It is often the small behaviours which support the more meaningful patterns of behaviour. For example, the dinner ritual won't work if the table is not set or the journals can't be found, as I learned the hard way!

We constantly refer to our family action list and if the children are not working as a team, I may have them write out the list and review its importance with me in what we call 'a family meeting'. The importance of the list is not so much about rules per se, but rather about working as a team, demonstrating family values and achieving rewarding goals. It's just like I said about my three ways of feeling happiness. This list helps us feel happy by encouraging those feelings of comfort which come part and parcel with cooperation. It also brings us happiness through having engaging relationships as we work together and having rewarding goals, such as finishing this book. We all enjoyed the anticipation of imagining what life would be like when the book was completed. In some ways, our action plan is like our family creed. This is how it goes.

Fenton family action plan: Operation Happy Family

Our values:
- team
- family
- loyalty
- cooperation
- empathy and compassion
- gratitude
- resilience.

Our beliefs:
- We apply ourselves to the enjoyment and purpose of this moment
- We can achieve anything as a team with dedication, practice and resilience
- We embrace all people without prejudice
- We do not define ourselves by the opinions of others
- We define ourselves.

Our attitudes:
1. Always move forward rather than backward
2. Smile, be kind and care
3. If we want to achieve, we need to be a team and stick to our plan.

Our actions:

1. Journal every day for ten minutes (goals, gratitude and daily review)
2. No clutter means more happiness
3. Plan one comforting activity each day
4. Keep our rooms clean
5. No dirty or clean clothes on floor
6. All communal areas left tidy and ready for clients, friends and family
7. Toilet paper replaced with empty roll put in bin, not on floor
8. Care for animals because they can't take care of their own needs
9. Have a daily plan ready and written out the night before in diary or journal
10. Be ready for the next day on the night before (uniforms laid out, homework completed, etc.)
11. Wash your dish
12. Bath or shower daily
13. Keep the shoe cupboard tidy
14. Never ever, ever eat away from table
15. Keep kitchen clean all the time
16. Let Mum work and we will all benefit
17. Leave the bathroom ready for the next person
18. No rubbish to be left out
19. No games covers, controls or disks to be left out
20. Close doors and cupboards
21. Lights off at night, use salt lamps instead

22. No shoes upstairs
23. Never leave anything personal in kitchen
24. Never leave makeup, toothbrushes or brushes out in downstairs bathroom
25. Leave nothing on bathroom benches
26. Cat not allowed downstairs.

When I read back over this list it occurs to me that there are quite a few 'nos' and 'nevers' running through it. Essentially I like to feel positive and focus on the 'yes' in life, especially as we learn. But in order to do this, we need to be crystal clear about our boundaries, so that every 'yes' has the space to flourish and we can all become the people we wish to be. Think about how you might adapt or create a similar action list for your family or maybe just for yourself. What would you put on it? What actions would help uphold your attitudes, beliefs and values?

When there is no time to tend the garden

Plant rituals are important. My garden admittedly went a little wild during the writing of this book, but I still tended my pot plants and this gave me much happiness and a sense of well-being. When there is no time for you to garden or life is throwing hardball, understand the situation, forgive yourself and decide which plants you will tend. My outdoor garden may be wild but the five pot plants in my bathroom are doing well and this small rainforest gives me so much comfort.

Always remember your dreams

There are so many stories throughout history of people suffering adversity who in the end found a way to survive and even thrive. Sometimes it is necessary to pass through a stage of loss, grief or difficulty, but what matters is that you keep believing in yourself. In whatever way you can, honour your values, practice your rituals and observe your self-talk. Create the space you need to be yourself and always follow your dreams. I say this to you from my heart and also from my experience. I cannot begin to tell you how many times I wanted to give up on this book. I could not count the number of times people have stared in disbelief when I have said that I am writing a book about happiness. Towards the last days of writing this, a colleague's mother asked me what I was doing. I answered that I was writing a book about how to be happy. She burst out laughing and said, "What a joke! You, writing a book about happiness." On this occasion I felt self doubt and sought counsel from Anita. Her response was "She doesn't know you but I do. I have taken the time to listen to you and to hear you. I know the book will be great, and you know this also." Wise Anita is right. My friends, always believe in yourselves and never allow someone else's opinion to become your own. Instead, surround yourself with people who know you, accept you and support you just as you are.

Find support

As a YouTuber, personal trainer and podcaster, I am in contact with a lot of people. I receive many letters daily, yet out of all the people who have crossed my path, I have possibly five soul friends. For me, a soul friend is like a soulmate. These are the special few who want me to be the real me, and when I am with them, I feel like I can be myself, warts and all. I am so lucky to have these friends. They are not your run of the mill friends. They would leap over tall buildings and be there for me in a moment. In fact, I know they would accept calls from me in the middle of the night, drop everything and rush over to help me. Never would they have any judgment and always they encourage me to be myself, but despite these wonderful, willing, giving friends of mine, I still seriously struggle to ask for help. It is, as I've already indicated, one of my greatest limitations.

After my marriage ended, I continued to tell myself that I could 'do it all' but I can't. In fact, no one can. Fortunately, my friends were there to help. Anita, Tara, Victoria, Denise, Leigh, my cousin Lona, Mum, Dad and so many others. These are people who do not judge but just get the job done. It is true that being ok with asking for help is something I am still learning, but even so, I encourage you to ask for help when you need it. We all need support and your friends are a great source this, but be sure to choose them wisely. The term 'friend' is not one to be used loosely. I encourage you to think about and define what friendship means to you. You can write about this in your journal. Note down the behaviours you believe friends would ideally demonstrate and reflect on the people in your life who uphold these values and actions. This is not a list of people to whom you flippantly make yourself vulnerable. These are people you trust over time for good reason. Treasure them because they truly are blessings in your life.

Exercise 1: Your contingency plan, break glass list and support list

I want to pause for a moment before continuing on with the strategies you can use to sustain your ritual practice, so you have a chance to implement the ideas we have already discussed. Your task for this exercise is to create your own contingency plan, break glass list and support list to help you when your practice gets put under pressure. As you make your plan, keep in mind the reasons you practice your rituals and think about the circumstances when you might need a contingency plan or break glass list. We do these things ultimately to keep us feeling happy and to give us systems to practice that happiness. By creating your rituals, you are literally devising a series of exercises to teach your brain to flex its happy muscle. Designing a contingency plan and support list is part of this process, and the best part is that it is tailor-made for you.

Some of you might find making these plans and lists a bit challenging. I have already let you know that I struggle to ask for help. Are you like this too? What are your limitations? What are your strengths? What sorts of things might prevent you from sticking with your ritual practice and what systems can you put into place to make sure that your rituals happen? What do you need in a crisis? Brainstorm your responses in your journal. The crises you write about could range from planning a celebration without any money to keeping your commitment to have a date night or family dinner even when it feels like you have no time for it. The key here is to acknowledge your strengths and weaknesses, as these are what will help you manage and understand the difficulties you may face. Let's start with your strengths. Write down ten of them in the space provided below. An example of a strength might be *I never give up* or *I am resilient*. If you are struggling to identify your strengths, ask a trusted friend or family member what they think. Don't just take them at their word, though. You need to feel the truth of that strength for yourself.

Strengths

1

Chapter 5

2
3
4
5
6
7
8
9
10

Now for your weaknesses. This is not an invitation to get negative about yourself. It is simply a recognition of certain areas where you may need to do a bit of work. An example is *I sometimes don't ask for help and try to do too much by myself.*

Weaknesses

1
2
3
4
5
6
7
8
9
10

Contingency plan

Equipped with your list of strengths and weaknesses, I want you now to write a couple of paragraphs about the systems you could put into place to allow your rituals to continue through the hard times. Think of all the things that might disrupt your rituals and remember to refer to your core values here. Make your plan practical and specific. It is designed to be used, so it needs to work. Elements of your plan may include:

- Knowing your purpose and values
- Identifying and assessing the risks
- Planning for what could happen and having a response ready
- Prioritising what matters
- Maintaining your values and being happy.

Break glass list

This is for desperate measures. Again, drawing on your strengths and weaknesses, write down a list of break glass resolutions. What actions can you take to make sure you hold on to the essence of your rituals? What adaptations can you make to the details so you focus on the meaning? Look back through my list above to see if that sparks any ideas for your own.

Support list

For this part of the exercise, I want you to refer back to your journal and your reflections on the meaning of friendship. Make a list of people you trust and who are likely to provide help when you call on them. You might like to note down next to each name the kind of assistance they can provide (e.g.

Chapter 5

running an errand for you, fixing a leaking tap) or the situation in which you would call on them (e.g. when your confidence is low and you need encouragement, when you need a good laugh or when you have run out of patience). Make sure to include all relevant contact details for the people on your support list. You might like to make a few copies of this list so you always have one handy. Simply seeing those names and knowing these people are prepared to help will bring you feelings of comfort and reassurance.

What value did you find in this exercise?

My response: *I really loved this exercise as I found writing the book really tough at times and definitely needed to have a contingency plan and break glass list. Through exploring my contingency plan and relating it practically to my core values, I found that anything became possible.*

Your response:

_____
_____
_____
_____
_____
_____
_____

What did you learn from this exercise?

My response: I learned that even the act of preparing a contingency plan helps me to feel comfort and increased my sense of anticipation of reward. By planning, I not only felt a greater sense of self, but I could clearly visualise and maintain my rituals.

Your response:
_____
_____
_____
_____
_____
_____
_____

Make yourself accountable

I have said before that happiness can only be experienced in the present. It is the same with the decision you make to be accountable. The only time you have to start anything is now, so don't procrastinate. What systems can you put into place to ensure the job gets done? I love the SMART goal setting formula (Doran, 1981). This is an acronym for goals that are smart, measurable, achievable, relevant, and time referenced. SMART goals:

- S   Have a specific purpose
- M   Are measurable to show when they have been achieved

CHAPTER 5

A   Are achievable and attainable because they are clearly defined

R   Are realistic, possible and practical given the available resources

T   Are achieved within a set timeframe.

Our rituals are much like this SMART acronym, don't you think? Actually, you could say that if rituals are not SMART, they revert back to being simple habits. In order to make rituals possible, they also need to be SMART. Now, my intention here is not to turn this into a goal setting or time management section but for you to understand that accountability and systems can help support our rituals and help them to occur habitually. Are your rituals SMART? Can you use the SMART system to refine them? The SMART-er they are, the more likely you will learn to feel happy by practicing them.

One great thing about using the SMART system for your rituals is that it can help make you more accountable for your happiness. The system encourages sustainable achievement, which is what this chapter is focused on. Another good strategy for creating accountability is to have a buddy. I use my three friends as accountability buddies. When I walk with Anita, I talk about my goals and directions, and we touch base with each other to ensure we are where are where we promised we would be. We refer to the SMART system and explore our values. I also train with Victoria and Anita to keep my mind clear and my body healthy, and I meet with Tara to discuss parenting ideas. I guess you could call them my SMART buddies. Their encouragement, suggestions and affirmation help make sure that I stay on track.

Time management

A vital part of ensuring that our rituals are practiced is to manage our time. This also fits in with the SMART formula. I keep a Google diary with alarms and an app on my phone. Each day, I check the diary against my goals. I enjoy ticking these off when I achieve them. I make sure to acknowledge my successes and pat myself on the back. I check the diary at the same time each day to ensure that I stay on track. When I am aware that I am procrastinating, I practice the art of noticing and reflect on why I am doing so. I use the following approach. You could call this a time management ritual.

1. I use Google tasks to keep a list of daily tasks to achieve
2. I keep a Google docs template of all my goals, together with staged steps which need to be achieved by particular dates
3. I keep a journal which I write in for short periods so that regular journaling is achievable
4. I use a diary which I keep beside my chair and check every morning and night for things like bills that need to be paid, school notices, and doctor's appointments
5. I use the task alarm on my iPhone so that I will not forget particularly important tasks
6. When I am out of the house, I sometimes send myself emails as reminders
7. I never look at emails unless I have the time to process them, because I get so many that if I didn't employ this approach, I wouldn't get through them with any resolution or system.

Throughout this process, I work towards staying in the

present and remembering my core values. I value my time and get great satisfaction out of planning my day in the present, as well as working towards future goals. I really enjoy checking, ticking off, reviewing and acknowledging my achievements. Every night before bed and first thing in the morning, I plan my time. I find the practice of planning time comforting and means that I am much more likely to achieve my goals which also makes me feel good. When we allow time to escape us, we also allow moments during which we could feel gratitude, compassion and resilience to elude us. When time escapes us, in a way so does happiness.

Rituals for accountability

Can you think of a ritual you could design that will help keep you accountable for your happiness practice? You could devise a time management ritual too, like the one I have. Perhaps you could share or practice your rituals with a trusted friend, or seek out your own accountability buddy. This could be a fun form of engagement for you and you will also get the reward of both giving and receiving support. Remember that the role of an accountability buddy is to keep you on task with encouragement, honesty and compassion. And of course, you will each be there to celebrate the other's achievements.

Learn acceptance

You know how it is. Some days it just feels like everything that can go wrong has gone wrong and it's only getting worse from there. These are the days when we really struggle not only to hold on to our ritual practice, but also to keep our composure and not get sucked into a negative downward spiral. I remember one day in particular that was like this. I was trying to get everyone to school on time so I could catch up with my writing for this book. In the preceding weeks, my son had been sick with gastroenteritis, my daughter had asthma and then both of my boys had bladder issues (yes, one after the other.) After all of that was over, I finally set aside a day for myself to get stuck into some uninterrupted work.

I got the kids ready for school and went to drop the boys off. When we got to the school gates, my son told me he had forgotten his bag. We went home and got the bag and I took him back to school. That's when he said he had forgotten his money to pay for school photos. I knew this was really important to him, so back home we went again, got the money and again I drove him to school. Just as we arrived, he burst into tears. I asked him what was wrong and he said, "Mummy, I forgot to put my shoes on!" We had driven all the way from home to school and back again twice and he did not have any shoes on. I could have got angry or upset at all the time this had taken, but instead I just laughed. I laughed and laughed and laughed.

It is often said that laughter is the best medicine. Well, I say laughter is the best ritual. It can help us accept the messy truth of our lives with good grace, and it can support us when our rituals get derailed. Sometimes we just have to accept that our practice isn't perfect and we are not either. That doesn't mean we give up. We can still practice being happy. Just going through the motions of happiness can make a difference to our mood. If we treat ourselves gently and with kindness, we will find it easier to accept when things don't work out the way we want them to. Likewise, if we smile, we might just find that before long we do feel a little bit lighter and a little bit happier. It's that old saying about fake it until you make it. Even if you have to pretend to begin with, accepting yourself and your circumstances will mean that you can find your way back to your rituals with less stress.

Get perspective

Acceptance and perspective are like two sides of the same coin. It is hard to have one without the other. When we accept our lives as they are, we gain perspective. When we have perspective, we are better able to accept our lives. I have mentioned already how just a short meditation each day can help keep anxiety at bay. Can you see how important both acceptance and perspective are to this? Once again, it comes back to our way of seeing. We can let ourselves get caught up in gossip and judgement, or we can decide to see things in a different way. It is like climbing up to the top of a mountain and looking down at the view. With practice and grace, we can choose to see the bigger picture and realise that however painful or imperfect our current experience might be, there is still meaning and beauty in it.

Letting go of rituals

This chapter has been about how to maintain your ritual practice. Would it surprise you if I now said there is definitely a time to let go of rituals? Your rituals are there to provide you with meaning. Once they stop doing that, they have served their purpose and it is time to let them go. If you find you feel tired or overwhelmed by trying to complete your rituals, then consider letting some go. The rituals are to help you feel not only happy, but calm and connected as well. Keep in mind what is possible and understand that it may take some time before you find a way of practicing that is right for you. Our lives are always changing, so our practice must change too. Don't be too hard on yourself about this. Just keep implementing the skills of seeing, noticing, reflecting and practicing that you have learned along your journey and you will be fine.

Exercise 2: Objective observation

Time for a reality check. Sometimes when I get too caught up in things, my inner child's voice takes over and I find I am calling myself a weird loser and other unkind names. Does that happen to you too? Every now and then, we need to step outside our usual way of seeing things and undertake some objective observation. That's what this exercise is designed to help you do. It invites you to reflect on what is happening with your practice and identify what's working and what's not, with support, empathy and recognition.

What I would like you to do is to write a letter to yourself as if you are a caring friend. The idea here is that this friend would see you (the reader of the letter) more sympathetically than you can yourself, and could recognise and name your many good qualities and efforts. The friend knows your strengths and admires them, and knows your weaknesses and accepts them. She or he would encourage you to feel resilient and to keep going in difficult times, and would also be able to acknowledge which of your rituals are working and which are not. Furthermore, your friend will remind you of your values and suggest ways for you to stay on track. This letter from your wonderful, caring friend is specifically about your ritual practice and how this relates to your happiness. It will talk about how your rituals are comforting, promote engagement and are rewarding, and it will expresses compassion and offer support. Doesn't that sound like a letter you would really like to receive? Then get writing, my friends!

What value did you find in this exercise?

My response: *I loved this exercise. I found that it is easy to offer someone else support and compassion, but not so easy to provide it for myself. By being the friend here, essentially for myself, I was able to see my situation more clearly and hence the importance of my rituals for my own happiness.*

Your response:

_____
_____
_____
_____
_____
_____
_____

What did you learn from this exercise?

My response: *I learned that a virtual situation, such as writing yourself a letter, has the power to comfort, provide engagement and is rewarding. I realised how much power I have in my own mind to train myself to feel happy.*

Your response:

_____
_____
_____
_____
_____
_____
_____

A quick check in

How did you go with that exercise? It is a powerful one, isn't it? I felt quite emotional when I read my own letter to myself. It can be so easy for us to lose sight of the good things we do in the busyness of our daily lives. That is when having the support of good friends and the ability to reflect become so valuable. That is the message I hope you have got from this chapter. I also hope you have found the strategies I have suggested useful. Which ones resonated with you the most? Which ones do you think you will put into action? Are you feeling more confident about your ability to keep practicing your rituals? I hope so. I just have one more piece of advice for you about this. In some ways, you could say that I have saved the best until last.

It all comes back to meaning

Yes, my friends, it's true. It all comes back to meaning. This is the real secret to maintaining and sustaining your ritual practice. As long as you keep your meaning in mind, you will discover that you can find a way to perform your rituals even when life gets tough. Let's remind ourselves again of the many different ways that rituals help us to feel happy. Rituals can:

- affirm our sense of self
- help us to acknowledge our worth
- remind us to stay present in the moment
- establish a feeling of belonging
- train our minds to focus on the positive
- allow us to experience feelings of happiness through comfort, engagement and reward
- invite us to become more aware of all of our senses
- encourage us to celebrate ourselves
- foster feelings of gratitude and compassion
- generate a sense of wellbeing
- enable us to create meaning in our lives.

Do you agree with the items I have placed on this list? Would you add, remove or amend any item and why? Remember that this journey is about your personal experience of happiness. All of these wonderful benefits and more come from practicing our rituals. Any time we feel our practice is slipping, we just need to remind ourselves of why it is so important to sustain it. This next exercise is designed to do just that.

Exercise 3: Remembering why

What is great about this exercise is that not only do you get the benefit of reminding yourself of the purpose and value of your rituals, but you also have the opportunity to revise or revisit any rituals that no longer carry the meaning for you that they once did. To start with, have a look at the map you made in Chapter 4 of all your rituals. Notice without judgement which ones you are performing regularly and which ones you are not. Now write down a few lines about the meaning each ritual on this map has for you. Don't just assume that this meaning will be the same now as it was when you first created the ritual. Your relationship to the ritual and the significance it has for you may have changed as a result of practicing it. If you are struggling to identify the meaning of any of your rituals, make a note of that too. It may be that you need to alter these rituals somehow to bring the meaning back into them. Or perhaps it is just time to let them go and create space for new ones to emerge.

Take some time with this exercise to really explore the deeper meaning behind each one of your rituals. Through doing this, you may feel a stronger sense of affirmation. You might even discover that some of your values are not being expressed through your current rituals. With everything you have learned so far, you can adjust and adapt your practice, letting go of rituals that no longer serve you and creating new ones to further enhance your happiness and sense of self.

What value did you find in this exercise?

My response: *The value of this exercise is that it keeps my rituals meaningful, relevant and achievable.*

Your response:

_____
_____
_____
_____
_____
_____
_____

What did you learn from this exercise?

My response: *I have learned that rituals are practiced to train our mind to focus upon and feel the meaning which we give our lives and that meaning brings happiness.*

Your response:

_____
_____
_____
_____
_____
_____
_____

Ritual to acknowledge your progress

You have grown so good at creating your own rituals. This is an opportunity for you to design one more. It may be that this is a ritual you do less often than some of your others. You might even feel the need to do it only once. It is completely up to you. The only condition for this ritual is that it enables you to acknowledge the wonderful progress you have made. This could be done as a meditation, a mantra, a reflection, or you could even devise a special ceremony. Use your imagination and create something that is filled with meaning. You have achieved so much through your dedication to improving your happiness. Make this ritual one that recognises your achievement.

In a nutshell

There are so many strategies in this chapter to help you maintain and sustain rituals for happiness every day. Here is your quick reminder of some of the key ideas we have covered:

- Rituals are vital to our wellbeing.
- We will all face challenges in our practice of rituals, so it is important to develop strategies to keep practicing them even in difficult circumstances.
- Making our rituals more habitual means we can focus more on the meaning behind them and less on actually getting them done.
- It is a good idea to make a contingency plan for times when you find it hard to keep up with your rituals.
- Don't be afraid to seek help and support from those you trust.
- Find ways to keep yourself accountable, such as using the SMART strategy with your rituals.

- Accept that your practice may not be perfect.
- Getting perspective on yourself and your practice will allow you to focus on the meaning of your rituals and remain flexible about how you enact them.
- It always, always comes back to meaning.
- If your rituals are not making you happy, change them.

There is just one more chapter left to go and it is a good one. It's all about celebration, so get ready to have fun.

Chapter 6
CELEBRATE YOUR PROGRESS

IT IS A Wednesday in September and I am smiling. A big, happy, crow's feet grin stretches from ear to ear and I am definitely in the mood for celebrating. I have finished a final draft of my book and sent it off to my editor, and today I am meeting with my mum and dad and aunt and uncle. We are gathering to celebrate my graduation with a Masters degree in Counselling from Monash University. In the months after my marriage ended, I enrolled in this course, thinking that it might provide the answer to me being able to financially support four kids. It was not long before I realised that the practical responsibilities and commitments which come part and parcel with caring for four young children really precludes full-time employment, but this degree has opened my eyes to the ideas of cognitive behavioural therapy and the process of changing your thoughts to change your mind.

I have been looking forward to this day for some time and have visualised it in my mind. For me, this anticipation is part of the celebration. It is like imagining the taste and aroma of a piece of hot apple pie before biting into it. I know that my family are proud of me and love me. My aunt is likely to bring a beautiful, symbolic gift. My father will make a speech and my uncle will say, "Well done, kid", as he always does. My mum will hug me and tell me that she loves me, as she always does. My dad will behave as if I am the smartest person he knows, even though I think he is the smartest person I know. Throughout my life, it has been so important to me to please my dad and he is delighted to express this pleasure. As my dad grows older now and has less mobility, my love and respect for him continues to grow.

Finishing this Masters course is a significant moment for me. Not only was it a personal achievement that I set myself, but I completed it during a particularly difficult time. This is an area in which I have wished to study for most of my life. I've learned so much and I am grateful for that. I am so glad, too, that my book is nearing completion. Today is an acknowledgement of all the work I have done, but it has been a team effort too. My children and friends have supported me through this process. The kids were awesome (most of the time!) and so many girlfriends came by to have chats, make suggestions, listen to me read from different chapters, give me feedback and support me with encouragement when I wanted to give up. This book has represented thousands of hours of thinking, writing, sorting and redrafting over a 16 month period. Now, I am celebrating all of that effort in my favourite way, which is to share a meal with people I love.

We are having lunch at the Wheelers Hill Hotel in outer Melbourne, which has a beautiful outlook towards the Dandenong Ranges. I chose this venue deliberately, because I used to serve tables here when I first attended university in my early twenties. At that time, I had no idea what I wanted to do or be. I did an Arts degree, majoring in Anthropology, because my lecturer told me I was good at Anthropology. I had no real direction of my own back then. I just wanted to be told that I could do something, or anything. So this is a special time and a special place for this celebration. The hotel is symbolic of me coming full circle and my family are here to witness this. We sit at the table, smiling and enjoying each other's company. My dear aunt. My uncle. My mum and my dad. I can feel their love and pride in me and I can feel it from within myself too.

As we lift our glasses, I think back over my journey. It is not just the writing of this book and the completion of my degree that I recall. Nor is it all that has happened since my marriage ended and everything that occurred during the years I was married. It is the whole story I reflect upon now, right from the time when I was that unsteady toddler learning to read, through to the girl who had such a vivid imagination and was bullied at school, and on to the teenager who learned that exercise was the way to free her mind, and at last to the adult Lauren who finally learned that being different is not a shortcoming but a strength, if you choose to see it that way (and I do.)

I think about my children and how their lives have changed mine. I think of the richness and wonder and mayhem they have brought to my being. I reflect on who I am and what I value and how I share these qualities with those around me. I think of my rituals and how they bring such meaning and structure to my days. My smile widens when I think about the fact that I am now inviting you, my dear readers, into this practice and all the benefits it brings. I pause for a moment and focus on my breath. I notice how my body feels. It is brimming with gratitude. I have so much to celebrate. So, so much. I let myself sit in this moment. I look at the loving faces around me and take a sip of my drink.

Yes, I am happy. Happy I am.

CHAPTER 6

Reflecting on your journey

Being happy is not easy. You knew that when you first picked up this book and you know it is true now. Sometimes it just seems so much simpler to sit like a frog in the mud and croak "I give up" or "I can't". It takes a lot of courage and resilience to pick yourself and keep on going, but that is precisely what you have done. I am so proud of you for that. This chapter is all about celebrating your progress. You did this. You have read this far into the book, you completed the exercises, you kept a journal and you explored your sense of self. And now is the time to celebrate. We will explore the three important facets of celebration, which are to reflect, rejoice and reward. You'll be invited to reflect on your journey, rejoice in your achievements and reward yourself for all you have learned. How do you feel about the progress you have made? What are your achievements so far and which areas do you feel that you could keep working on? When you look back on your journey, what stands out for you the most?

This whole adventure started with the idea of beginning where you are. We then discovered the importance of self-awareness, self-understanding and self-acceptance to our happiness, before discussing ways to create the physical, mindful and social space for good things to flow into our lives. Next, we learned more about rituals and developed some of our own. We created a practice of daily rituals for happiness for ourselves and learned how to maintain and sustain this practice, even in difficult times. Now we are on the home run and we have a lot to celebrate.

Why it is good to celebrate

When you think about it, many of our social and cultural rituals are to do with celebration. Think about Christmas and birthdays. Think about graduation ceremonies, like the one I mentioned above. Celebrating is about observing and respecting an important occasion with particular practices and positive sentiments. But it is also more than that. Celebration is really about enjoying and being in the moment, not just for ourselves, but to help others have a sense of belonging. Our celebrations make us feel good but they also remind us of who we are and what matters to us. They give us a sense of belonging and a recognition of our accomplishments. Often, our celebrations are shared with people in our family or community, but sometimes they can be more private too.

There are many reasons to celebrate. I like in particular to celebrate resilience. When the kids have managed an incident of bullying or have made it through a difficult test, we will acknowledge that by going on a group activity, like skateboarding or seeing a movie. Like so much that we have learned in the pages of this book, a lot of celebration has to do with both the art of noticing and our way of seeing. When we notice what is around us and what is happening within us, we can find so much to celebrate. When we choose to see what we do as an achievement, we can see many occasions for celebrations. Just as we have discovered techniques to train our minds to experience happiness, so we can shift our focus and our behaviour to allow more celebration in our lives. And of course this can in turn further increase our happiness.

This is because celebration tells our brains that we have done a good job. We are rewarding ourselves for our efforts and acknowledging our worth. This is very important for a strong sense of self. Through celebrating certain behaviours, we also increase the chances for such behaviours to become more internalised and habitual. There is really a lot more to celebration than just having a good time. To understand this, let's begin by considering the importance of reflection. I want to start by telling you a story. It is about reflection, but it is about food and family and celebration too. Do you want to hear it? Pour yourself a hot cuppa and pull up a chair.

Reflect

Honestly, I don't know how I survived my childhood without ending up the size of a house. There was just so much food! Dad loved food to excess and as a child, I just accepted this without question. My sister lovingly called our family get-togethers 'pig outs'. Traditional Polish food and my dad's incredible enthusiasm for it were a normal part of my daily life. These are memories I now hold as so precious. Every Sunday after church, my dad took over the kitchen. He made spaghetti carbonara and kluski and potato salad. We would arrive home and Dad would start enthusiastically cutting up onions and bacon. Whatever quantities were required, I am sure he doubled them. He would go to such an enormous effort to make the carbonara and there was always so much of it. He would mix cream cheese with the bacon and onion and serve it with so much spaghetti, plus rye bread and lots of butter. The more butter the better. Once we sat down around our huge table, we would make the sign of the cross and say grace in Polish: *W imię Ojca, i Syna, i Ducha Świętego*. Then we would all eat while he talked. Throughout the meal, I would catch him constantly looking at my mum like she was something so special that if he stopped looking, she might disappear. He has been like that with my mother for over fifty years now.

Dad was so proud of how much I would eat and he would

share this with everyone without discretion, as if it were a badge of honour, much to my grandmother's disgust. As a frugal and humble survivor of the Depression, my grandmother, who we lovingly called Noni, was at times a little horrified by my dad's exuberant ways. My grandmother would often say 'waste not, want not' and place a recycled ice cream dish under the tap to stop water wastage. She used to shake her head vigorously at my father, which secretly I think would egg him on to greater feats of theatre and exuberance. Even so, my father's large smile and his desire to dominate all conversation as he sat at the table are among my favourite memories. He made every meal a celebration, but it was not until I was writing this book that I realised the real reason my father always wanted us to have 'too much' food. In the conclusion, I share more of my father's beautiful story. And with his story, mine too makes more sense.

It was only through the reflection that was necessary for me to write this book that I have realised how wonderful my childhood actually was. Before the book, I focused on my learning difficulties, my experiences of school bullying, my clumsiness with people, and my marriage ending. Growing up, I also resented having had such an isolated Christian upbringing (although I now view this as a loving protection rather than isolation.) I blamed my parents for not educating me about lifestyles that were different to ours. Attending university in the 1980s was in some ways a shocking experience for me. Rebellious punk and Goth fashion with piercings and safety pins were 'in', and remember this was a time before the internet, mobile phones and reality shows. It was a time when students would attend rallies, go to the pub daily for lunch (and often not return to class), and party hard. It was a very different style of living to the one I was used to.

To give you some idea of what it was like, I first attended

Chapter 6

Monash University in Clayton, Victoria in 1983. This was a time of heavy student political activism and recreational drug use. Heroin, cocaine, and LSD were prolific. Students were romantically idealistic and sexually exploratory. They enjoyed pushing conservative boundaries and many were left wing. Marijuana was openly smoked in what was then infamously called the 'small caf'. I remember the staff going on strike on one occasion, saying that they could not work in such conditions. Nelson Mandela was in prison, the Berlin wall was up, and apartheid still reigned. Students were idealistic and questioned everything with gusto. Into this tumult I came with my Polish, orthodox Catholic background, and my belief in God, traditional family values and fidelity. Although I had many friends at university, there were a few who didn't like my strong Christian beliefs and practices. I was ridiculed, my conservative values were laughed at, and I was called unrepeatable names referring to my Catholic values. I consider the names I was called too graphic and obscene to repeat here, but some students wrote them over my books.

On one occasion, male students stuck electrical tape all over a favourite library desk and my books, with words inferring that the only way one could have physical interaction with me was by force. (I am changing the language here so it is more acceptable for the reader.) I wanted to fit in so I did not report these students. Today, I would have taken police action and said exactly what I thought. I would have asserted myself. But in those times I felt shy, insecure, and had so much self doubt. Consequently, I felt at times some resentment that my parents did not warn me about the harsh and cosmopolitan world outside our family. My father was constantly concerned for my safety and asked that I did not read negative media articles in the paper. He just wanted me happy. I see now the enormous effort my parents put into our family life. I see their passion, their challenges and their care. I also now see the value of their perspective. My parents have given me an amazing blueprint for happiness, for which I thank them. But it is also important that we develop our own way of seeing and making sense of the world, and indeed that we take responsibility for ourselves, and this is where reflection comes in. I am sharing these stories with you in the hope that you may learn from them. Belonging is important, but only if you remain true to yourself, assert your needs and demonstrate your values. It is never ok for someone to bully, control or scare you. I want you to know that.

What experiences of this have you had? Have you ever been rejected or ridiculed by your peers? And how did you choose to reflect upon and acknowledge these experiences? How do you process your not-so-positive experiences? Do you carry these as emotional baggage by wallowing in them and feeling resentment like I did like I did? Or do you learn from these encounters? Sociologist Jack Mezirow (1997, p. 5) says that "A defining condition of being human is that we have to understand the meaning of our experience. For some, any uncritically assimilated explanation by an authority figure will suffice. But in contemporary societies we must learn to make our own interpretations rather than act on the purposes, beliefs, judgments, and feelings of others."

The key words here are "understanding the meaning of our experience". I believe that we understand the meaning of our experience by unpacking it, processing it and reflecting upon it. Through doing this, we learn more about ourselves. We develop self-awareness and we gain perspective. There are so many stories in our lives and so many entwined threads of experience, feeling and emotion. When you look back, which threads are you going to remember? Which experiences are you going to allow to shape your way of seeing? Will they be

Chapter 6

happy ones, like my memories of meals with my family? Or will they be hurtful ones, like the times we were called names or when our relationships fall apart?

When I reflect upon my marriage today, I remember the beautiful property we lived on. I remember the yoga room and the lovely dinners and conversations I had with my dear husband at the time. I remember his wildly gesticulating arms when he told a story and how people would gather around to listen when we went out to dinner. I remember his impassioned love of gardens. I am so grateful that I met him as we have four beautiful children. These are comforting memories for me now, but it has taken work and a conscious decision to focus upon the value of that time in my life. Just because we have something for a finite time and it comes to an end doesn't mean we have to remember the whole experience as negative. Yet it is only as a result of writing this book that I have been able to reflect like this and find some peace with it. The writing has allowed me to look back and find happiness. I now feel so grateful to my ex-husband for giving me those experiences.

There is a difference between reflecting upon our experience and carrying with us baggage from the past. Part of that difference lies in our way of seeing, but it also can be found in our ability to celebrate. Through reflection, we can learn to appreciate ourselves and our lives. And through celebration, we show respect for the people we are and the journey we are taking. When we celebrate, we allow ourselves to make not only meaning but also joy from our experiences. This is something I have really come to see about myself and about happiness in general. I wonder what it is you will see when you take the time to reflect on your journey. What discoveries have you made? What perspectives have changed? Wouldn't it be interesting to find out?

Exercise 1: Reflecting on your happiness

Do you remember the first exercise I asked you to do, all the way back in Chapter 1? It was to fill in a questionnaire about your current beliefs and experiences of happiness. Now, I invite you to fill it in again, only this time I want you to head to your happy space and spend some time meditating first. During your meditation, focus on becoming calm. Let yourself feel gratitude and compassion. Let go of any worries and reflect on your journey with a smile. Then, when you feel ready, you can complete the questionnaire. Resist the temptation to look back at your answers from Chapter 1. Only when you have filled in this questionnaire a second time do I invite you to compare your results. As before, consider each statement carefully and indicate how much you agree or disagree with it according to the following scale:

1. = strongly disagree
2. = moderately disagree
3. = slightly disagree
4. = slightly agree
5. = moderately agree
6. = strongly agree.

Feeling comfort

1. *I feel happy most days.*
2. *I smile every day.*
3. *I engage in hobbies or interests which I enjoy.*
4. *I have daily rituals which I enjoy.*
5. *I have a sleep routine and I sleep well.*
6. *I eat a balanced, nutritional diet.*

Chapter 6

7. At the end of the day, I feel peaceful.
8. I am aware of experiencing comforting moments throughout the day.
9. I enjoy my daily walk or exercise.

Empathetic and engaging relationships

1. I have several friends who I am close to.
2. I participate in my community.
3. I feel fortunate to have the relationships that are currently in my life.
4. I have boundaries and can say no if necessary.
5. I attend family celebrations and enjoy these occasions.
6. I enjoy meals at the table with friends or family each day.
7. I give to others.
8. I don't hold grudges.
9. I feel compassion for the people in my life.
10. I have several habits I repeat which give me a sense of connection with others.

Experiencing rewarding goals

1. I set rewarding and achievable goals.
2. I make time for meaningful things in my life.
3. I enjoy the present moment and don't get distracted.
4. I embrace change.
5. I acknowledge my achievements and make sure I celebrate them.
6. I have habits I repeat each day which I find rewarding.

7. *I manage and structure my time.*
8. *I enjoy planning, anticipating and working towards my goals.*
9. *I enjoy consciously reflecting on happy times.*
10. *In most ways, my life is just the way I want it to be.*

Self-awareness
1. *I know my strengths.*
2. *I accept my weaknesses but continue to work on them.*
3. *When I make mistakes, I review them realistically, adjust my behaviour and move on.*
4. *I am happy with what I have now.*
5. *I make time each day to practice mindfulness, through prayer, meditation or simply being in the moment.*
6. *I rarely find my mind wandering.*
7. *I let go of negative experiences fairly quickly.*
8. *I don't ask for reassurance or worry about what others think of me.*
9. *I have rituals which give my life meaning.*
10. *I feel grateful for my life every day.*

How did you go? Did you learn anything new about yourself this time around? Did any of your answers change from when you first completed this questionnaire at the beginning of the book? What does this say about the journey you have been on? If you like, you could reflect on these questions in your journal in addition to answering the two questions below.

What value did you find in this exercise?

My response: *I found this exercise incredibly valuable as it gave me a map of the areas in which I need to improve my practice. It is also a window into the areas in which I struggle to let go. I personally will redo this questionnaire each month. I think it is vital to use my answers to support my happiness and self-awareness, rather than to see them as a numerical pass or fail. Life is ever evolving and we are only who we are any moment in time. We are a product of how we choose to interpret each experience, reflect on that experience and learn form that experience. I choose to practice happiness.*

Your response:

_____
_____
_____
_____
_____
_____
_____

What did you learn from this exercise?

My response: *I learned how the practice of ritual and taking time to notice the beauty in each day and enjoy ordinary things has improved my ability to feel happy every day. I have learned about my own happiness but also about my ability to notice and practice skills in happiness, and my beliefs about it.*

You response:

_____
_____
_____
_____
_____
_____
_____

Rejoice

Just as there are many reasons to celebrate, there are many ways we can do it too. A key ingredient in any celebration is rejoicing. To me, this means a feeling of lightness and pleasure, when all of my senses are attuned to delight. When it flows from reflection, rejoicing also includes an element of appreciation. I think we can experience joy more deeply when we take the time to consider the real cause for our celebration, which is almost always some kind of growth or change. I am sure you already have a number of favourite ways to rejoice, either on your own or with others. Here are some ways that I like to do it.

Laughter

I have a funny laugh. Yes, I admit it. My laugh sounds a bit like a machine gun or a kookaburra. I have a very large mouth and when I was young, I would try not to laugh as the other kids would tease me. Now, however, I laugh with my mouth wide open and just swallow up the moment. Laughter gives us such a great feeling of joy. When we laugh, we are really in the moment. We can't think about other things because we are so caught up in our laughter. In fact, one of my sisters used to laugh so much that she would faint from lack of breath!

It is really, really, important to our happiness (not to mention our sanity) to be able to laugh even, or perhaps especially, when things get hard. A big part of both happiness and rejoicing lies in your ability to hold on to your sense of humour, to laugh, smile and turn a difficult situation into a joke. I also think that part of the art of noticing includes being able to notice the humour that is around us every day. Start looking out for it and you'll find yourself laughing and rejoicing more and more.

Sing and dance and stamp

Sometimes there is nothing better than letting yourself get swept away by a giddy, childlike feeling of delight. You know that sense of euphoria that makes you want to shout with joy? Let yourself feel it! Let yourself shout. Sing or dance or stamp your feet. Play in the mud and dance in the rain. Be like my exuberant dad calling out his love to my mum in the shopping centre. My dad has always, to this day, expressed the inner child within him, and we each have benefited from that childlike joy. Express your joy in whatever way feels good to you. Just relish those wonderful, positive emotions.

Smile

Did you know that how often we smile is an indicator of how long we might live? Ron Gutman (2011) did a sensational video on this topic. He talked about how one smile has a greater effect on the pleasure centres of the brain than 2000 bars of chocolate. Isn't that amazing? After I watched that video, I made a conscious effort work on my smiling. I found that as I smiled more at my children, so they smiled more at me. Then I started smiling at people when I was shopping or out and about, and they also would smile back at me. This in turn affected how I felt, which brought more smiles to my face and caused more smiles from my children, and so the ripples went on and on. This just might be the simplest happiness ritual of all. Smile. Do it when you're happy, but do it when things get tough too. Do it just because, and do it for no reason at all.

I have learned and gained a lot from my smiling practice. At home, we have started a weekly reward for the child who smiles the most. We even keep a chart. This was of course a little tongue in cheek (excuse the pun), but what we found is that everyone benefits from the experience and the person who wins each week gets to decide on a fun family activity for us all to share. It was interesting to see how once one of us started smiling, it became contagious. Before long, it was like the lyrics of that Frank Sinatra song and the whole world smiled with us. The wonderful Buddhist teacher Thich Nhat Hanh says "Sometimes your joy is the source of your smile, but sometimes your smile can be the source of your joy." Why don't you try it out for yourself? In your journal, write a list of things which bring a smile to your face. Notice for one day or even one hour how many times you smile and then consciously try to increase that number. How does it feel to smile more? What responses do you get from others? How does this practice impact on your level of contentment, peace and happiness?

Gratitude

You knew I was going to mention this one, didn't you? That is because I believe it is so important to feel and express our gratitude every day. David Steindl-Rast (2013) says grateful people are joyful people, so let your gratitude and joy show. Take time to think about how truly lucky you are right now and then give thanks. Sing, stamp, dance or shout your gratitude out to the world, or do it more quietly and just smile. However you choose to do it, rejoice in your good fortune. We are, all of us, really so very lucky.

Hugs

I have never been a hugger. In fact, as a child I hid behind the couch rather than hug people. But as I have grown, I have learned about and experienced the power of the hug. Now I love to hug my children good night. The thing about hugs is that it is the giving rather than the receiving which counts. Hugs can give us a feeling of comfort and of belonging, but did you know they can also lower our blood pressure and cortisol levels? Sometimes when we are rejoicing, we just want to share our happiness with others. A hug can be a good way to do that. It's simple but it makes a difference.

Ceremonies

When my marriage first ended, my children created a number of ceremonies in order to remind me of their love for me and to affirm our sense of being a team. Often they would record these ceremonies on video. We now watch them and laugh as the kids were so young back then and they took the ceremonies so seriously. On one occasion, they brought me out into the garden and, in an effort to cheer me up, said that they had prepared a ceremony for me to marry one of their toys. They had gathered flowers in baskets and had each carefully prepared a speech stating my importance and telling me how much they loved me. It was so touching. Another time, the kids created a ceremony to invite friends to join our family, a bit like an adoption process. These ceremonies all required elaborate preparation, recording for posterity and an expression of love. They are very special memories for me.

Celebration often has an element of ceremony to it and sometimes these ceremonies can be serious, but they can be fun as well. Indeed, it is possible to design a ceremony where the focus is all on rejoicing. The great thing about ceremonies is that they really can be made to include a whole family or community. Everyone can have a role to play and everyone gets the benefit from participating. What ceremonies can you think of that are like this? What kind of joyful ceremony would you like to see?

Exercise 2: Rejoice with happiness ceremony

This is a really fun exercise. Let this bring out the child in you to indulge in some childlike fun. You get to create your own ceremony to rejoice with happiness. Start by making a list of ten ways you might celebrate. This could including anything from dancing to skydiving. Just list whatever is joyful and meaningful to you. Next, think of the elements you want to include in your ceremony. Do you want food or music as part of it? Perhaps a scripted speech? A symbolic lighting of candles or flower petals strewn across the pathway? Will it be held in a special place? What time of day or year will it happen? Who will you invite and what role will they play? Have fun with these details, but remember that the focus of your ceremony is on rejoicing, so don't let it get too complicated.

When you know what you want to do, start to plan out the finer points of your ceremony. You could do this through visualisation or meditation, or you might write about it in your journal. Make sure that you identify which values are being celebrated in your ceremony too, and use the SMART principles that we explored in Chapter 5. When you have made a plan for your ceremony, I want you to perform it. Gather together the people and materials you will need for it. Make it a special occasion and make sure you have fun. That includes enjoying the delicious experience of planning and anticipation.

What value did you find in this exercise?

My response: *This exercise helped me see that the value of goals and celebration can be found in the anticipation and planning as well as the event. Life is about enjoying the journey, not just arrival at the destination.*

Your response:

_____
_____
_____
_____
_____
_____
_____

What did you learn from this exercise?

My response: *I have learned that ceremonies and rituals can allow me to bring out the child in me, and to have fun and laugh. Rituals can be fun.*

Your response:

_____
_____
_____
_____
_____
_____
_____

Reward

The third important facet of celebration, after reflection and rejoicing, is reward. These rewards do not need to be anything too grand. Sometimes a simple treat is better, as long you associate it with the reason for the celebration. I set up regular rewards for my family. Often these are occasions when we go out for hot chocolate or on picnics or take a trip to the skate park. We reward ourselves by spending time together in the sunshine. I also reward myself at times with some creature comforts, such as candles or incense and nice towels. Even a cup of my favourite brand of tea can be a reward, or putting a few drops of lavender oil on my pillow. These rewards are all cheap, accessible and possible, but the best thing is that I get to enjoy them more than once. First, there is the anticipation. I get to enjoy the journey towards the reward, whatever that may involve. I like to visualise myself moving closer to whatever goal I have set and I really imagine the sensations I will feel when I finally reach my reward. The reward is never about achieving the goal. It is about the motivation and the work you do towards it. Every time I buy a lottery ticket, for instance, I visualise how I am going to spend my winnings. I envision how much I would enjoy spending that money on travel, sharing it with people and setting up projects. Even if I don't win (which is what usually happens), I have still loved the dream and the imagining of my wealth.

Next, there is the pleasure of the reward itself, however simple it may be. I bring all of my attention to the experience of the reward. I give the moment the respect it deserves and I let myself celebrate it. Finally, there is the recollection of the reward. I can reflect on it in detail, savouring the sensations and the feeling of satisfaction and accomplishment. Daniel Kahneman believes that how we remember our experiences is an important component of our happiness. He says "our lives are governed by the remembering self. Even when we're planning something, we anticipate the memories we expect to get out of it" (Spiegel Online International, 2012). It is like that with rewards and with celebrations. We can feel happiness from anticipating, experiencing and remembering them.

Exercise 3: Reward yourself

This exercise encourages you to feel happiness in each of the three stages described above. You will start by choosing a reward for yourself. This may be in recognition of a particular goal you are seeking to achieve or it could be a way to celebrate your commitment to increasing your own happiness. It could also be a treat you choose to give yourself just for being you. Remember to make sure your reward is possible and accessible. Try to work within a small budget as this is not about money but rather about experience. When you have decided on your reward, spend some time in your happy space visualising it. Focus on the sensations you will feel when you reach this reward. Imagine it in detail and enjoy the anticipation of it. Then, at a suitable time, give yourself your reward. To make this more special, you might like to include it as part of a ritual or ceremony. Let yourself really feel the sensations of appreciation, delight and gratitude for your reward. You have earned it so enjoy it. Later, in your journal or in a meditation, reflect on your reward. Look back on the whole journey you have been on and you will see that there were rewards in it for you the whole way through.

For me I have planned to have a glass of champagne and a cake when I finally hand in this draft. I am going to light a symbolic candle and say "I am ok. I knew I could do it". I will use the words "I am ok", as these words precede many of my rituals. I am also going to hug each of my children and invite my girlfriends over. I will drink up the sensations of being together and of experiencing gratitude for the moment. I will acknowledge the resilience I showed in managing to pick myself up countless times through adversity and get this book done. I think about this moment often and I smile each time I visualise it. When it happens, I will take pictures of the moment so I can reflect upon the day I completed my book, which is to be the first of several. I will also make a little speech to my family about my journey and how it feels to achieve the final draft.

What value did you find in this exercise?

My response: *The value I found in this exercise is that it shows both the power of visualisation over our frame of mind and also the importance of celebration as a ritual part of rewarding ourselves for our achievements. It is valuable to identify the various parts of the ritual, as well as to use symbols to highlight the importance of loving engagement.*

Chapter 6

Your response:

_____
_____
_____
_____
_____
_____
_____

What did you learn from this exercise?

My response: *I have learned that it is not just the reward of celebration which is important here, but walking through life imagining, visualising and believing in the reward so that every day can be experienced as a celebration.*

Your response:

_____
_____
_____
_____
_____
_____
_____

Rituals of celebration

I hope you are feeling excited by all the different ways you can celebrate. At the end of this chapter you will find one last, very special ritual that is a way to commemorate your journey of discovery through the pages of this book. Before we get there, though, I want to mention one or two other ways that you can bring together the ideas of ritual and celebration. The first is through mantra. I recently had a client who, after making great progress towards happiness and balance in his life, was concerned that he would fall back into old habits. For him, that involved overworking without meaning. I set him the homework task of writing his own daily happiness prayer or mantra. You can use the same technique as a ritual to reflect on and rejoice in your progress. Like a compass, you can also use it to keep you on course each day. A mantra can be a word or a phrase which is repeated while you focus upon a higher meaning such as gratitude, compassion, or belonging. It might also be a set of phrases much like a poem. An example might be something like this:

> *As I walk the journey of my life, I celebrate at the start and end of each day.*
>
> *I celebrate my relationships with a smile and with my hands outstretched.*
>
> *With each step I feel grateful and compassionate.*
>
> *At times I fall, but I find opportunity and resilience in my fear.*
>
> *I reflect upon my life and feel calm.*
>
> *I let go of the past, sit in the present and embrace the future.*
>
> *I am happy daily.*
>
> *As I experience each moment, I celebrate happiness.*

Another way you can connect ritual and celebration is through something similar to what my family did when we decided to honour our decision to commit to being happy. Here's what happened. As a family we came together around the table. We put away all distractions and dedicated ourselves to the ritual. We lit a candle and held hands. We spoke our commitment out loud to each other and dipped our hands in sea water as we said the words. Then we reflected in silence on our decision. Afterwards, we congratulated each other and promised to support one another. We hugged and then closed the ritual by blowing out the candle. You might choose to do something like this too. You have learned enough about rituals now that you can find some special way to include celebration as part of your practice. I want to tell you again how proud I am of you for how far you have come. Rituals are not easy. They require constant application. By adding celebration to your ritual practice, you may find more motivation to keep going and more compassion for yourself when you stumble. You will also be acknowledging your own worth, which is something most of us could afford to do more often, don't you think?

The Christmas story

From all the stories I have told you in this chapter and in the whole book, you will know that celebration is really big in my family. My sister especially loves to celebrate and she puts so much effort in to our family gatherings through videos, photos and ceremonies. We often refer to her as the 'family glue', as she is so adept at bringing us together with such loving and symbolic rituals. Secretly, I think she would have made an amazing caterer. While the rest of us are often too busy, my sister somehow always manages to get it done and is always thinking of others. Her gifts are amazing and her approach to

Christmas has kept our traditions going for years beyond what I would have done if I had been running things. I really admire her for that. I love her for her empathy, her organisational ability, and her sense of family. On one occasion when I was financially struggling and embarrassed to speak about it, my sister rang around local butchers who donated sausages to our family. When I reflect upon this, I think about how much guts and determination and courage that would have taken, especially when she has her own children and pressures. Another time she turned up with a car full of groceries. I am so grateful to her for her empathy.

One Christmas, about four years ago, I was in the position when I just could not afford to purchase any reasonable presents for my children. Most years are a struggle, but this time around, the situation was worse than usual. I didn't know what I would do. My dear mum bought us a tree and some decorations, and we received a generous donation of food and a hamper. But there was still the issue of the presents. Eventually, after much thought and planning (and lots of private tears behind closed doors), I created a dream box for each of my children. The boxes were large and full of tissue paper so the kids would have the fun of rustling through them to find the small, symbolic treasures nestled within. Each of the four boxes contained a pencil and a journal, along with specially selected items which reflected that child's infinite potential.

My younger daughter's box held a Russian doll, which symbolised her quest to find her inner self. Each of my boys found in their boxes little figurines of dragons coming out of eggs, which reflected my belief that my children could become anything that they want to be. My eldest daughter received a mask and a watch and a few other small items. Also in the boxes, there was a letter with a quotation and an explanation of each item. A little while ago, I asked my daughter if she remembered what was in her box. She rushed straight to her room and brought out that letter. This is what it said.

Maya's dream box

"Dare to live the life you have dreamed for yourself. Go forward and make your dreams come true."

- Ralph Waldo Emerson

Maya,

You are a talented, beautiful, imaginative, compassionate, fit, goals-oriented little girl. I love you with all my heart.

I have given you a mask in your dream box because you have the ability to be whoever you want to be. You have the power to decide your identity and your destiny. I am so excited to see how your future unfolds.

I have included a watch in your box, because in order for you to achieve your goals, you will need to manage your time and set realistic goals to achieve. Every action you take, whether intentionally and unintentionally, will bring you either closer to or further away from your goals, so choose your actions wisely.

II have included a gem-like bracelet, as to me you are a gem full of light and potential.

I have included an elephant because I want you never to forget how special you are and what you can achieve.

I have included an eraser so you can remember that each failure brings us closer to our next success.

I have included an anklet that you can wear and touch to

remind you to stay in touch with who you are and what you are going to achieve.

I have included the crystal citrine to help you attract the abundance and potential that you not only deserve but can create. Citrine has been called the stone of the mind. People in ancient cultures believed that placing citrine on the forehead of an elder would increase psychic powers.

I have included a book in which you can list all your goals so that you never lose sight of them and will take steps to make them real.

I have included a rainbow pencil so you can write these goals in all the colours of the rainbow.

Go forward, Maya, and make your dreams come true.

I love you so much,

Mum

(Christmas 2012)

I thought at the time that these dream boxes meant little to my children, as they each had a wish list of toys and presents that was well beyond what I could afford. But we still talk about that Christmas today. In some ways, despite having no money, it was one of our best Christmases ever because the gift of the dream boxes showed my kids how much I loved them. As they often do, my children have received many presents from different people over the years. With time, they have tired of and abandoned many of these gifts, and yet my daughter kept this present of her dream box in a special place and knew exactly where it was when I asked about it. What I thought meant so little actually meant so much. Yes, once again, my dear friends, it all comes back to the meaning behind the action, behind the symbol, behind the celebration and behind the ritual. If you have learned nothing else from this book (and I sincerely hope you have), then please remember this. It is all about the meaning and how we choose to experience and express that meaning in our lives.

Ritual for reflection, commemoration, celebration and potential

This is it. This is the last ritual in this book and it is a really special one. What I want you to do is create a dream box for yourself as a way to celebrate both your arrival at this point and your potential beyond this moment. Choose a few small items of symbolic significance, together with a quotation or mantra that is meaningful to you. Place these items in a box or arrange them somewhere like an altar. These items symbolise who you really are, along with your infinite possibility. When you have chosen these objects, write yourself a letter explaining the meaning behind each one. Congratulate yourself for who you have become and honour the potential that is within you. Make a commitment to yourself to look from time to time at the items in your dream box or on your altar. Reflect on the wonderful journey you have been on and acknowledge your dedication to your path. Be grateful. Be content. Be happy.

In a nutshell

We are almost at the end of this part of our time together, my friends, but before we get to the conclusion of the book, let us recall the important messages in this chapter.

- Celebrations are important because they are about honouring important occasions and reminding us of who we are and what matters to us.

- There are many reasons to celebrate if only we learn to notice them.
- The three key facets of celebration are reflection, rejoicing and reward.
- We understand the meaning of our experience by unpacking it, processing it and reflecting upon it. When we do this, we are better able to appreciate and celebrate.
- Laughter, humour, singing, dancing, stamping, smiling, gratitude, hugging and ceremony are all wonderful ways for us to rejoice.
- Rewards can be enjoyed through anticipation, experience and reflection.
- Adding celebration to our rituals can give us more motivation, compassion and acknowledgement of our own worth.
- And, as the story about the dream boxes shows, it is always, always about the meaning and how we choose to experience and express that meaning in our lives.

In the final part of this book, I reveal more of my father's story. It is quite a tale, let me tell you. I am looking forward to sharing it.

Conclusion

The end of the story

(for now anyway)

I have great memories.
I am a happy man.

My dad – Leonard Ostrowski

MY FRIENDS, WE have finally reached the end of the book. Instead of breathing a sigh of relief as I thought I would, I find myself feeling a little wistful. I feel like it is I who has become the reader, now seated beside you, rather than the writer of these words. Through reflection, writing and my own process, I have watched my story of happiness unfold in front of me. In a way, I feel some sadness that it has come time to complete these last pages. This experience has completely changed me. I no longer feel lost or broken. I feel calm and comfortable with who I am. And I feel resilient. I know that I am capable of change. I know that life can be hard, and I choose to feel happy anyway. Yes, I feel content.

I initially thought that it was the end of my marriage which brought me pain, and I held this experience to me like I was protecting a gaping wound. But with time I realised that it was my lack of self-awareness and self-acceptance and my fear of change that were the true cause of my pain. It was only after I made the decision, following the first draft of this book, to candidly write about my childhood that the words started to flow cathartically. With the words came self-understanding and then the dam broke, and I found both perspective and detachment. It was as if a burden had lifted. I felt so sad for little Lauren who was abused by her teacher, but with the new insight I acquired, I was able to let her know that it was not her fault, and she could be anyone she chose to be. Then I found I could feel compassion for that wounded teacher too. Perhaps you might find it difficult to understand how I could feel compassion for a teacher who was abusive, but I know that her unkindness came from a place of her own hurt. And how do we break that cycle of viciousness unless we understand, accept and then forgive? I forgive her. And with my forgiveness comes my self-acceptance.

Recalling and releasing my childhood through the writing of this book has brought me peace, not only about the experiences that occurred then, but also about many other events that have happened throughout my life. At the age of seven, I chose to allow my experiences of difference and judgement to affect my view of myself and my worth. This in turn affected how I internalised my experiences. Seeing my world differently has given me the perception to realise that happiness is my choice, and it is within my control. I now view my life and myself differently, through compassionate and peaceful

The End Of The Story

eyes, and I feel happy. But make no mistake, my friends, it has been my daily exploration of ritual which has opened the door to this new way of seeing. It has been through the dedicated practice of certain rituals that I have affirmed my values, reminded myself of who I am, become more grateful, and ultimately gained perspective.

Before I started writing this book, my way of seeing was that of a bullied child who had been misunderstood, marginalised and judged by many who met her. My perspective was full of self doubt, some bitterness, and mistrust. As I reflected through my writings and research, I discovered that I have so many wonderful memories alongside these harsher ones. They were always there, of course, always part of my story and of my journey. I just did not take the time to notice these memories and look at them with realistic optimism. If I had been able at the time to be aware of what was happening, rather than realise it only later through reflection, I would have seen the love my parents have for me. I would have been able to honour my own incredible gifts and talents, and cherish the countless wonderful moments I experienced. I do feel happy now, but it is with a new realisation that I have actually been happy all along.

The truth is that I started this journey because I wanted to find a way of protecting myself from further pain. What I have learned is that I am responsible for my own happiness. I now know that being different is something to be proud of, that family and friendship is everything to me, and that compassion and gratitude are the windows through which we must view our world. All I needed in order to realise this was the space to see my life in a fresh way. I needed the space created by distance, the space created by journaling, the space created by meditation and reflection, and the beautiful space given to me through my practice of rituals. In a lot of ways, writing this

Conclusion

book has given me the space to be me, and through all of this, I feel as if you have been sitting here beside me. You have always been in my mind as I was writing and as I was selecting which stories to share and deciding which exercises and rituals would be most useful and enjoyable for you. I hope you have found them valuable. I hope you have learned as much about yourselves as I have about myself. I thank you so much for listening to my story and for sharing in my experiences and my rituals of happiness. I really want to thank you for taking this journey into self-discovery and self-development with me.

I have said at several points throughout this book how wonderful and amazing my parents are. In this conclusion, I want to speak more about my dear dad. It is fitting that I speak about him here at the end of this journey, because the happiness that ritual has brought into my life and yours is all thanks to him. He is the one who introduced ritual to my life. I have so many treasured memories of my father, from his effusive protestations of love for my mother across the supermarket aisles, to the trips to St Kilda for feasts of cakes, to teaching me my times tables, to the huge servings of spaghetti carbonara on Sunday, to the focus he has always placed on resilience. Among the many things he has taught me are to hold onto family and to never give up. These are lessons he himself learned the hard way through the experiences of his life.

Let me share a little insight into my dad's particular way of seeing the world. Like me, he was born into a loving and close family. This was in Warsaw, Poland. He says, "I had an idyllic childhood. My life really was paradise. The days were sunny and I remember my father telling me to be honest in all things" (Robinson, 2007, p. 9). But in September 1939, when he was just four years old, my father's peaceful life crashed to pieces when Hitler's army invaded Poland. "My happy childhood got knocked for six," he says (Robinson, 2007, p. 9). "I recall being held in my father's arms, cuddling up close to my mother. It was night time. They were looking at a beautifully red glow in the sky, listening to distant explosions, and saying 'Warsaw is burning'" ("Judge Ostrowski bids adieu", 2007, p. 40).

My father's next memory was of the Germans storming into his "idyllic childhood" home and seizing everything. "I recall being massively surprised that my father did not throw them out. Surprised that he looked helpless" he explains ("Judge Ostrowski bids adieu", 2007, p. 40). His family was evicted and forced to live in lodgings without a bathroom. His two brothers had disappeared. Food was scarce and he was alone as a six year old boy for a lot of the time. Dad remembers feeling hungry and sleeping on a mattress that was infested with bugs. He was covered with sores and his skin would bleed. He remembers that at this time his father brought him a small wooden horse with wheels. He talks of that horse to this day. He was only six years old and had been in hiding without consistent family for a year, often going without food and always living in fear. The next time he saw his father was when he was lying in a coffin surrounded by candles. He remembers hearing people praying and his mother, who he loved dearly, dressed in black. She held his hand as they walked slowly behind the horse-drawn hearse and as she sobbed at the edge of the grave.

Death was common in Warsaw then. My dad remembers seeing young men being lined up against the wall in the streets and getting shot (Robinson, 2007). I wonder at times what it would have been like to be a little boy and to witness bodies suddenly crumple lifeless to the ground. My dad's family helped in the AK Polish Underground. He dearly wanted to join the Underground but, much to his dismay, was told at the age of six that he was too young. In early August 1944, Warsaw was cordoned off so that no one could enter or leave it. Sitting without food in his family's derelict apartment, my father

CONCLUSION

listened to the rattle of machine guns outside. It was the start of the Warsaw insurrection, the day that the Polish people rose up to stand firm against the Germans.

On another occasion, my dad says he "heard cries for help from the street pavement. We tied a couple of brooms together and passed them out into the road. The person hung onto the end and we dragged him in. It turned out to be my 12-year-old mate, with one of his legs shattered, and his shinbone sticking out at a right angle to the rest of his leg" ("Judge Ostrowski bids adieu", 2007, p. 42). My dad and members of his family spent weeks hiding in a cellar while the surrounding buildings were pounded by artillery. While still in the cellar, my dad turned nine. There was no celebration or rejoicing, no singing of 'Happy Birthday', no cake, no candles to blow out, no colourful gifts to unwrap, and no laughter. The family huddled in fear in a cellar, surviving on a mixture of flour and water. The measure of my father's fear can be gauged by the way he reacted when the first shell hit. Although reluctant to share his childhood experiences, my dad said to me recently when I read out this chapter to him, "I don't think you understand the level of fear I felt as a young boy." He then added: "Suddenly there was a loud explosion on the top floor of the building in which we were hiding. I felt the blast. Looking to the top of the stairs, I saw a dense cloud of something coming towards me. I yelled 'fire, fire, fire' hysterically and I leaped towards the ceiling window which was barred with iron bars. People were pulling me back and tried to comfort me, but I would have none of it, screaming, screaming again and again, 'we are on fire'. I was hysterical with fear." For five years now, they had been homeless, living with fear, famine and death.

I want you to understand that my father does not talk much of these times to me. He is a private man and prefers to live in the present. I found out these stories about him mostly

The End Of The Story

by searching through newspapers. By the end of my writing of this book, my father started to speak about his experiences. I remember as a child that my father had terrible nightmares at times, of which he would not speak. Sometimes now when I find my life is a little hard, I close my eyes and imagine what it would be like to be a little boy sitting in a squalid shelter in the dark with nothing but flour and water to eat, listening to the sounds of heavy artillery pounding outside. I imagine how that then seven year old boy would be feeling. How much more scared, how much more alone, how much more sad and lost would he be compared with me?

Eventually the Germans discovered the cellar where my father's family were hiding and they were all marched out at gunpoint. My father was separated from his mother and did not see her again for 25 years. Did you take that in? I know I struggle to comprehend it. My dad loved his mother and he did not see her for 25 years. He did not have her to attend his school assemblies or to be there on parent teacher nights. He did not have her to tuck him into bed at night with a story and a kiss. Now, with neither father nor mother, this little nine year old boy was herded like an animal with crowds of prisoners into cattle trucks for a journey lasting two weeks and eventually ending up in a camp in Landeck, Austria. Of that journey, he says: "Food was in short supply and the trucks so tightly packed that only some could sit while others had to stand. During this time we were allowed out twice" (Robinson, 2007, p. 9). It was now 1945 the war was over.

Dad was stateless and without any documentation. He could not return to his mother in Poland, but he was lucky to have his sister and brother-in-law who managed to care for him. Several people dear to him died around this time. It was not only Warsaw which was lost to him. The comfort and reassurance of his mother's soothing cuddles and the strength and guidance of his father's wisdom were also gone. As a refugee, he was taken to Switzerland and later immigrated to Australia at the age of fifteen. In Australia, my father went to school. He worked in school holidays in a road gang on the streets of Altona to get himself through a law degree at Melbourne University, to which he won a scholarship. When I turned eighteen, Dad became a Victorian County Court judge. My dad's progress from working on the roads to sitting on the bench as a judge reflects the courage, determination and resilience of the Polish people. In his retirement speech delivered on 6 September 2007, Dad said: "The orderly, peaceful and predictable life in beautiful Australia, the company of friends … the love shown by a girl who agreed to marry me, all combined to allow me slowly to melt away the hatred which marred my life … I had become convinced that following the path of a tooth for a tooth and an eye for an eye leads to a community becoming both toothless and blind, not a very desirable state of affairs" ("Judge Ostrowski bids adieu", 2007, p. 43).

For his whole life, Dad has believed in the rituals of routine, justice and family. These gave him predictability and a framework for the type of orderly behaviour which helped him achieve his goals and set an example for his children. My father used the comfort and predictability of rituals to reintroduce love and stability into his life, and he bestowed these same gifts onto each of us kids. Dad lovingly brought to our lives what was so violently taken from his own. My wonderful dad turns 80 in the coming months. We plan on each bringing a traditional Polish dish and gathering to celebrate as a family.

These days, Dad struggles at times with health and movement can be a challenge. I ask him if he is happy and he always says without hesitation, "I am so happy." When I ask him why, he says, "I have family and I love your mother and every moment is precious. I have great memories. I am a happy

The End Of The Story

man. Yes, I am happy. I have a crowd of kids, I love your mum." I ask him if he believes in God and he answers, "Yes, I do. God is always present, but it is not the belief in God which is the moment of truth. It is the living and practicing as if there is a God." In some ways, the same can be said for happiness. At the beginning of my story, I reflected on how my mother would lovingly say to my father, *"Nie tak duzo"* (not so much). Perhaps now you can see why family feasts, cakes and togetherness are so important to a man who as a child lost almost everything which was dear to him. Perhaps now you can also see why Dad placed made such a ritual of our gatherings and special occasions. Too much carbonara, too much kluski, too many cakes, and so much laughter. Yes, these were happy times.

When my marriage first broke down, I could not sleep and often felt intense panic. Many times during those months, I would call Dad at five o'clock in the morning. He would always answer the phone with a tone that gave the impression he was already wide awake and calmly waiting for my call. I look back now and contrast my pain at that time with his experience in the cellar and the tragic death of several of his family members, including his father, along with his 25 year separation from his mother. I think I understand now what was behind his tone of voice when I called him. He didn't want me to feel afraid and alone as he had been. For my father, family was everything. His parents, not by intention, were taken away from him, so he made the decision to always be there for me.

The meaning both my parents created for our family through ritual, values and beliefs fans out like ripples on a lake, touching our extended family, our community and our friends. Although my sisters and brothers each have our own lives, we still contact Dad when we have a problem and he imparts his age old wisdom, which is always objective and reasonable. Most of all, my father and mother have tried to teach

Conclusion

me resilience and to always see the glass as half-full. That is not to say that my upbringing has been without incident. As with most families, there have been difficult times. My parents have stood by each other steadfastly as best friends through illness, tragedy and change. Each time there is hardship, they adapt with resilience, communication and love.

It is not until I started to write this book that I considered deeply how life has been for my dad. And as I wrote the book, I finally realised what my dad has given me. It is the key to happiness. It was always with me, just as his love and guidance have always been. I just had not seen it until now. I remember one occasion towards the end of my writing when I went to visit my parents. Dad was sitting in his favourite chair by the window, looking into the distance with an expression of pensive calm. My mother, always busy in the kitchen, looked towards him anxiously and asked him if he was alright. Their eyes meet with love across the room. No words were required; it was just a moment. Just one of many moments like this they share every day. Then she offered him a cup of tea and reminded him to take his medication.

That is how it is with my mum. Above all else, she has taught me in her no-nonsense manner not to be a victim and to get on with life. There have been moments throughout my life when I have felt overwhelmed by study, relationship loss or judgment. At such times, I have come to mother asking for reassurance and she has always said the same thing: "So what, Lauren? Why care what he is doing or what she is doing? Worry about what you are doing. Don't be a victim." It has been this wisdom which has carried me through life. Throughout the writing of this book, Mum has telephoned me and told me to "hurry up and finish it!" When I was struggling to finish and I found the telling of my own story especially hard, Mum simply said, "You know I love you, so sometimes I need to say things as a parent to help you. There is no use, you know, in me being a parent if I can't pass things on to my children, is there? Lauren, I think it is time that you let go of this book. Don't you think? It is time." And as usual, she was right. It was time to let go.

Time to say goodbye

So here I am, writing, at last, the final pages of this book, and it is time for me to say goodbye for now. I need to let go of this story so that you can learn from it and so I can start making ready for my next book. I'm looking forward to it already. It will be the next stage of my journey, full of new discoveries and insights for me and for you. Where once the end of my marriage felt like the end of my life as I knew it, I now feel that it was one of the greatest gifts for my personal growth. I feel so very lucky to have had that opportunity to grow. If it were not for that, I may not have written this book. It was a turning point which allowed me to reflect on my life and learn to be in the moment and enjoy the journey rather than wait until I reached the destination. I am grateful to my ex-husband for the relationship we had, for the time we spent together, for our four beautiful children, and for everything our marriage gave us.

At the beginning of this book, I was fixated by my marriage ending and was desperately seeking a simple answer to happiness. Now at the end, I can at last see that the answer really is simple. I have a happy life and I always knew how to be happy. I just had to take the time to notice what was there. I dearly hope, my friends, that this is what you have learned too. I hope that all your journaling, self-discovery, reflection, meditation, and above all the practice of your rituals has taught you this one simple truth, that happiness is really about the meaning we choose to create in life. If I could give you one piece of advice from my fifty years, it is this: don't miss out on the jewels of happiness you already have, even if you sometimes need to dig a bit to find them.

Now that we have read through all the chapters in this book and have completed all the exercises, now that we can reflect on our own lives a little differently and have learned to notice life with all its beautiful moments, I want to look once again at my six beliefs of happiness that I mentioned in the introduction. Let's touch base with how you feel about these beliefs now.

1. *Happiness is a state of mind* that you can only feel today, not yesterday nor tomorrow. What do you feel right now? Breathe in the glorious air. You are alive!
2. *Happiness is an individual, subjective experience*, which means that only you will know what happiness is for you. Just like my mum lovingly told me, "Never allow the behaviour of others to determine your worth."
3. *Happiness requires self-awareness*, and with awareness comes understanding, acceptance and development. Wake up to who you truly are, for when you open your eyes to your true self, happiness will be there waiting for you.
4. *Happiness may be experienced in three ways* and these are through feeling comfort, having empathetic and engaging relationships, and pursuing rewarding goals. Drink your tea, laugh with friends, practice your rituals and feel the reward which comes from anticipating realistic goals.
5. *Happiness requires a conscious decision and intentional action*, so make the decision to feel happy in

spite of, or perhaps inspired by, the events in your life. Just decide to be happy anyway.

6. *And finally, and most importantly, happiness takes practice.* Just like my early morning piano scales, if you want to enjoy the music of life, you must practice and practice until the music plays and you learn to appreciate every beautiful note. You can do it, my friends. I believe in you.

From your reading of this book, you know that happiness is not a miracle. It is not something we can desire or search for, because the moment we start searching, we deny the reality that happiness is a state felt from within. In the simplest terms, happiness is a decision we make about the way we choose to think, supported by tools and strategies that we use every day. This whole book has been about giving you a window into my journey towards happiness in order to give you the tools and strategies to create your own rituals and hopefully open your own window.

There are a lot of areas I have not explored here, such as anger, health and fitness, forgiveness and intimacy. These areas are also important to happiness, but there is only so much I can cover in this first book. I have a lot more that I want to share with you, but for now, I just want to say again how proud I am of you for reaching this stage. Imagine me sitting here with a smile upon my face. Remember what you have learned in each chapter, my friends, and please continue to question and explore the meaning behind your rituals to keep them relevant and reflective of who you are. Remember your core values. A big part of this whole process for me has been about practicing acceptance and compassion. The more I practiced acceptance and compassion, the more the pieces of the happiness puzzle fell into place. I hope you will keep bringing these same qualities to your rituals. I hope you will be happy every day. That is my wish for you.

A final word

There have been so many times during the writing of this book that I felt doubt and even stopped believing in myself. I have stopped creating consistent podcasts and videos in the last few weeks in order to concentrate on the book. I needed to get the message right so that I may share this with you. I have received so many letters from my YouTube viewers and podcast listeners saying they miss me. To all of you who wrote to me with these messages of support, thank you. Thank you for your patience and for understanding that sometimes we need the space to do one thing at a time. Getting this book finished has been one of the hardest things I have ever achieved. There were so many times that I felt I had no right to write this, that I wasn't good enough or that it was all just too hard. So many things got in the way of me finishing this book, not least of which was myself. But as my parents taught me – and as I hope I have taught you – I picked myself up and kept on going.

Despite the doubts and difficulties I faced, I have loved writing this book so much that in the end I really didn't want to stop. Each day I would sit down with a cup of tea and write. This experience has given both me and my children so much happiness. Towards the end, the children started watching the TED Talks with me and afterwards we would discuss how we could bring the learnings from those talks into our lives. This whole process has allowed us to take a big step forward in our happiness as a family, and the important thing for you to remember here is that I am not different from you. I have been able to find my way back to happiness and I know you can too. Perhaps you already have?

My friends, I want to thank you again, so very much, for being part of this journey and for sharing in my story. Daily rituals for happiness have been my doorway to a more meaningful and contented life, and they can be for you too. You can practice smiling more, laughing more and working through your issues with realistic optimism. You can learn to live in the moment, notice the beauty around you and reflect on life with a smile. You can create the space in your life and your mind to engage with others, appreciate the little things and gain perspective. Keep practicing your practice. If you attend to it and reflect upon it, it will always give you the feelings of comfort, engagement and reward that are the essence of happiness.

Remember, too, that everything begins and ends with our sense of self and the way that we choose to see our world, so don't let anyone else dictate these things to you. Like my mother says, "Become brave enough to be the only person in your life who decides who you are, how you feel and what you will do." This choice is available to every one of us in every moment of every day. Let the rituals you have created remind you of this and let them bring you happiness. You deserve it. We all do.

I know you can do it.

Love to you all,
Lauren

Acknowledgments

Writing this book was such a wonderful journey for me and has brought me a level of self realisation and much happiness. My discoveries throughout this process include learning to accept help, recognising the power of good friends and family, and understanding that I alone hold the power to 'get back up'. I have the key to my own happiness.

I acknowledge and am deeply grateful to my editor Caitilin of Artful Words (www.artfulwords.com.au)

Caitilin, thank you for your professional expertise and support. Thank you for helping me make Alby fly. Alby is short for Albatross which is our affectionate nickname for the book.

I thank my dear Aunt Denise and Uncle Leigh for coming in to support all of us when things were tough. And thank you to Lona for being there for me(countless times).

Thank you to all my friends for believing in me. There are too many of you to mention, but I want to give a special thank you to Anita, Tara, Erin, and Victoria.

Thank you to my viewers and listeners for your many letters of support. You kept me going when at times I doubted myself. I often feel when I write or record videos and audios that you are sitting there alongside me, having a cup of tea.

And thank you to my dear, beautiful children for your belief, love, and patience. Keep making your dreams come true. You can do it.

About The Author

A single mother of four children including twins, Lauren holds an Honours degree in Anthropology and a Masters in Counselling from Monash University, Australia, and has worked as a personal trainer, life coach, speaker, and meditation teacher for many years. She has a popular YouTube channel and presents a podcast called 'Being Well with Lauren'. In Daily Rituals for Happiness, Lauren candidly shares her personal experience of loss, childhood bullying, relationship challenges, and the many ups and downs of being a single mum. With humour and insight, she offers hope, support and practical advice to readers on their own journey. Her heartfelt and approachable writing style allows readers to feel like they are listening to a life story told by a good friend over a cup of tea

References, suggestions and more goodies for you

There are so many brilliant books and YouTube videos which have affected the way I see happiness. To come up with a list of them is kind of like asking me to pick a chocolate from a box of my favourites. Here are the references I used in this book, along with some other wonderful resources and inspiring TED Talks.

References

Achor, S. (2011). *The happiness advantage: The seven principles of positive psychology that fuel success and performance at work.* New York, NY: Crown Publishing.

Brown, B. (2013, June). Brené Brown: The power of vulnerability. [Video file]. Retrieved from http://www.ted.com/talks/brene_brown_on_vulnerability.

Cordeschi, R. (2002) *The discovery of the artificial: Behavior, mind and machines before and beyond cybernetics.* Dordrecht, the Netherlands: Kluwer Academic Publishers.

Crisp, R. J. & Turner, R. N. (2010). *Essential social psychology.* London: Sage Publications.

Csikszentmilalyi, M. (2004, February). Mihaly

Csikszentmilalyi: Flow, the secret to happiness. [Video file]. Retrieved from http://www.ted.com/talks/mihaly_csikszentmihalyi_on_flow/transcript?

Dalai Lama. (2009). *The art of happiness: A handbook for living*. (10th anniversary ed.). New York, NY: Riverhead Books.

Doran, G. T. (1981). There's a S.M.A.R.T. way to write management's goals and objectives. *Management Review, 70*(11): 35-36.

Emmons, R. (2007). *Thanks: How the new science of gratitude can make you happier.* Boston, MA: Houghton Mifflin.

Gladwell, M. (2004, February). Malcolm Gladwell: Choice happiness and spaghetti sauce. [Video file]. Retrieved from http://www.ted.com/talks/malcolm_gladwell_on_spaghetti_sauce.

Gilbert, D. (2004, February). Dan Gilbert: The surprising science of happiness. [Video file]. Retrieved from http://www.ted.com/talks/dan_gilbert_asks_why_are_we_happy.

Gilbert, D. (2005, July). Dan Gilbert: Why we make bad decisions. [Video file]. Retrieved from https://www.ted.com/talks/dan_gilbert_researches_happiness.

Gutman, R. (2011, March). Ron Gutman: The hidden power of smiling. [Video file]. Retrieved from http://www.ted.com/talks/ron_gutman_the_hidden_power_of_smiling.

Hill, G. (2011, March). Graham Hill: Less stuff more happiness. [Video file]. Retrieved from http://www.ted.com/talks/graham_hill_less_stuff_more_happiness.

Jacobson, S. (2013). Core beliefs in CBT: Identifying and analysing your personal beliefs. *Harley therapy counselling blog*. Retrieved from http://www.harleytherapy.co.uk/counselling/core-beliefs-cbt.htm.

Judge Ostrowski bids adieu. (2007). *Victorian Bar News*, 142, 39-43.

Kahneman, D. (2010, February). Daniel Kahneman: The riddle of experience versus memory, [Video file]. Retrieved from http://www.ted.com/talks/daniel_kahneman_the_riddle_of_experience_vs_memory.

Killingsworth, M. (2011, November). Matt Killingsworth: Want to be happier? Stay in the moment. [Video file]. Retrieved from http://www.ted.com/talks/matt_killingsworth_want_to_be_happier_stay_in_the_moment.

Lucas, R. E. (2008). Personality and subjective well-being. In M. Eid & R. J. Larsen (Eds.), *The science of subjective well-being* (pp. 171–194). New York: Guilford Press.

Lykken, D., & Tellegen, A. (1996). Happiness is a stochastic phenomenon. *Psychological Science*, 7, 186-189.

Malinowski, B. (1922). *Argonauts of the western Pacific: An account of native enterprise and adventure in the Archipelagoes of Melanesian New Guinea*. London: Routledge and Kegan Paul.

Malinowski, B. (1926). Myth in primitive psychology. London: Norton.

Malinowski, B. (1944). *A scientific theory of culture and other essays*. Chapel Hill, NC: University of North Carolina Press.

Malinowski, B. (1979) *The ethnography of Malinowski: The Trobriand Islands 1915-18*. Michael. W. Young (Ed.). Boston, MA: Routledge and Kegan Paul.

Mezirow, J. (1997). Transformative learning: Theory to practice. In P. Cranton (Ed.) *Transformative learning in action: Insights from practice* (pp. 5-12). San Francisco, CA: Jossey-Bass.

One Day University (2010). *Positive psychology: The science of happiness*. [Kindle version]. Retrieved from http://www.amazon.com.au/One-Day-University-Presents-Psychology-ebook/dp/B0049B2G1M.

Perls, F., Hefferline, R., & Goodman, P. (1977). *Gestalt therapy: Excitement and growth in the human personality.* (New ed.). Gouldsboro, ME: Gestalt Journal Press.

Ricard, M. (2003). *Happiness: A guide to developing life's most important skill.* New York, NY: Little Brown and Company.

Ricard, M. (2004, February). Matthieu Ricard: The habits of happiness. [Video file]. Retrieved from http://www.ted.com/talks/matthieu_ricard_on_the_habits_of_happiness.

Roberts, J.A., Tsang, J., & Manolis, C. (2015). Looking for happiness in all the wrong places: The moderating role of gratitude and affect in the materialism–life satisfaction relationship. *Journal of Positive Psychology, 10*(6), 489-498. doi: 10.1080/17439760.2015.1004553.

Robinson, R. (2007, October 6). Tough justice. *Herald Sun Weekend*, pp. 8-10.

Rutledge, R.B., Skandalia, N., Dayanc, P., & Dolana, R.J. (2014). A computational and neural model of momentary subjective well-being. *Proceedings of the National Academy of Sciences of the United States of America, 111*(33), 12252-12257. doi: http://www.pnas.org/content/111/33/12252.

Schawbel, D. (2013) Brené Brown: How vulnerability can make our lives better. *Forbes*. Retrieved from http://www.forbes.com/sites/danschawbel/2013/04/21/brene-brown-how-vulnerability-can-make-our-lives-better.

Seligman, M.E. (2010). *Learned optimism: How to change*

your mind and your life. North Sydney, NSW: Random House Australia.

Spiegel Online International. (2012) Interview with Daniel Kahneman: Debunking the myth of intuition. Retrieved from http://www.spiegel.de/international/zeitgeist/interview-with-daniel-kahneman-on-the-pitfalls-of-intuition-and-memory-a-834407-4.html.

Steindl-Rast, D. (2013, June). David Steindl-Rast: Want to be happy? Be grateful. [Video file]. Retrieved from http://www.ted.com/talks/david_steindl_rast_want_to_be_happy_be_grateful.

Tolle, E. (2004). *The power of now: A guide to spiritual enlightenment.* Sydney, NSW: Hachette Australia.

Wagner, J. (1973). *The bunyip of Berkeley's Creek.* Melbourne, VIC: Longman Young Books.

Wallis, C. (2005, January). The new science of happiness. *Time.* Retrieved from http://content.time.com/time/magazine/article/0,9171,1015832,00.html.

Suggestions

Brown, B. (2010). *The gifts of imperfection: Let go of who you think you're supposed to be and embrace who you are.* Center City, MN: Hazelden Publishing.

Dalai Lama. (2002). *How to practice: The way to a meaningful life.* New York, NY: Atria Books.

Ellis, E., & Dryden, W. (2007) *The practice of rational emotive behavior therapy* (2nd ed.). New York, NY: Springer.

Gilbert, D. (2006). *Stumbling on happiness.* New York, NY: Vintage Books.

Gladwell, M. (2009). *Outliers: The story of success.* London: Penguin Books.

Glasser, W. (1998). *Choice theory: A new psychology of personal freedom.* New York, NY: HarperCollins.

Lyubomirsky, S. (2007). *The how of happiness: A new approach to getting the life you want.* London: Penguin Books.

Rubin, G. (2009). *The happiness project: Or, why I spent a year trying to sing in the morning, clean my closets, fight right, read Aristotle, and generally have more fun.* New York, NY: Harper Collins.

Seligman, M.E. (2013). *Authentic happiness: Using the new positive psychology to realise your potential for lasting fulfilment.* New York, NY: Atria Books.

Seligman, M.E. (2012). *Flourish: A visionary new understanding of happiness and well-being.* New York, NY: Free Press Random House.

My favourite TED Talks

Achor, S. (2011, May). Shawn Achor: The happy secret to better work. [Video file]. Retrieved from http://www.ted.com/talks/shawn_achor_the_happy_secret_to_better_work.

Brown, B. (2012, March). Brené Brown: Listening to shame. [Video file]. Retrieved from http://www.ted.com/talks/brene_brown_listening_to_shame.

Csikszentmilalyi, M. (2004, February). Mihaly Csikszentmilalyi: Flow, the secret to happiness. [Video file]. Retrieved from http://www.ted.com/talks/mihaly_csikszentmihalyi_on_flow.

Gilbert, D. (2004, February). Dan Gilbert: The surprising science of happiness. [Video file]. Retrieved from http://www.ted.com/talks/dan_gilbert_asks_why_are_we_happy?

Gladwell, M. (2004, February). Malcolm Gladwell: Choice happiness and spaghetti sauce. [Video file]. Retrieved from http://www.ted.com/talks/malcolm_gladwell_on_spaghetti_sauce?

Gutman, R. (2011, March). Ron Gutman: The hidden power of smiling. [Video file]. Retrieved from http://www.ted.com/talks/ron_gutman_the_hidden_power_of_smiling?

Hill, G. (2011, March). Graham Hill: Less stuff more happiness. [Video file]. Retrieved from http://www.ted.com/talks/graham_hill_less_stuff_more_happiness?

Kahneman, D. (2010, February). Daniel Kahneman: The riddle of experience versus memory, [Video file]. Retrieved from http://www.ted.com/talks/daniel_kahneman_the_riddle_of_experience_vs_memory.

Schwartz, B. (2005, July). Barry Schwartz: The paradox of choice [Video file]. Retrieved from http://www.ted.com/talks/barry_schwartz_on_the_paradox_of_choice.

My creations

My YouTube channel: Lauren Ostrowski Fenton

http://www.youtube.com/user/laurenlouisefenton

My podcast: Being Well with Lauren

http://itunes.apple.com/au/podcast/being-well-with-lauren/id1030685050?mt=2

My website

http://www.beingwellwithlauren.com

My Facebook page: Lauren Ostrowski Fenton well being coach
http://www.facebook.com/laurencoaching/

My Twitter account

http://twitter.com/beremarkablenow